Praise for *Black Folktales*

MW00575905

People who are interested in genealogy will find *Black Folk Tales of the Muscle Shoals* a wonderful source of information, including census records of numerous Black families who are mentioned in the stories.

—June Reed, reviewer

Cobb and Walker reconstruct a lost history of men and women who built "the very foundation of the Muscle Shoals" but whose stories "were left out of the Alabama history books in most cases."…The interviews point to the uniqueness of the region in Southern history, including northern Alabama's affiliation with Appalachia, as well as the complex interactions between Black residents and the local Chickasaw and Cherokee people. The interviews, which are important historical artifacts in their own right, are supplemented by astute commentary by the authors, who conducted additional interviews and research during a subsequent tour of the region.

—*Kirkus Reviews*

BLACK FOLKTALES
of the
MUSCLE SHOALS

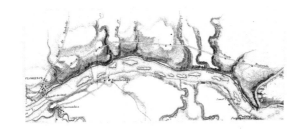

SLAVERY TO SUCCESS

RICKEY BUTCH WALKER AND HUSTON COBB JR.

ISBN: 978-1-958273-07-4 Paperback
ISBN: 978-1-958273-16-6 Hardback
ISBN: 978-1-958273-08-1 eBook

This work is based from the authors' personal research and interpretation.

Managing Editor — Angela Broyles
Interior Design — Katie Warren
Cover Design — Lamar Marshall

Bluewater Publications
books by Rickey Butch Walker

Appalachian Indians of the Warrior Mountains: History and Culture, ISBN 978-1-934610-72-5, $24.95

Appalachian Indian Trails of the Chickamauga: Lower Cherokee Settlements, ISBN 978-1-934610-91-6, $24.95

Black Folktales of the Muscle Shoals, ISBN 978-1-958273-07-4, $24.95

Celtic Indian Boy of Appalachia, ISBN 978-1-934610-75-6, $24.95

Chickasaw Chief George Colbert, ISBN 978-1-934610-71-8, $19.95

Cotton Was King - Franklin – Colbert County – Alabama Plantation Series, ISBN 978-1-949711-08-0, $24.95

Cotton Was King - Lauderdale County – Alabama Plantation Series, ISBN 978-1-934610-99-2, $24.95

Cotton Was King - Lawrence County – Alabama Plantation Series, ISBN 978-1-949711-14-1, $24.95

Cotton Was King - Limestone County – Alabama Plantation Series, ISBN 978-1-949711-35-6, $24.95

Cotton Was King - Morgan County – Alabama Plantaion Series, ISBN 978-1-958273-03-6, $29.95

Doublehead: Last Chickamauga Cherokee Chief, ISBN 978-1-934610-67-1, $24.95

Hiking Sipsey: A Family's Fight for Eastern Wilderness, ISBN 978-1-958273-11-1, $24.95

Soldier's Wife: Cotton Fields to Berlin and Tripoli, ISBN: 978-1-9582730-98, $19.95

Warrior Mountains Folklore, ISBN 978-1-958273-02-9, $24.95

Warrior Mountains Indian Heritage-Teacher's Edition, ISBN 978-1-934610-27-5, $39.95

Warrior Mountains Indian Heritage-Student Edition, ISBN 978-1-934610-66-4, $24.95

Acknowledgements

I greatly appreciate the valuable assistance of Yolanda Morgan Smith in completion of this book. She is my go-to person for census, marriage, and death information.

I also wish to thank my sister, June Reed, for editing the manuscript of *Black Folktales of the Muscle Shoals*. She also wrote the review for this book, and I greatly appreciate her help.

I really appreciate Lamar Marshall for working on and developing the cover of this book. Lamar has been a long time friend, and I thank him for his valued assistance!

I am especially thankful to Mr. Huston Cobb Jr. for providing his interviews for this book. Without his information, the quality of *Black Folktales of the Muscle Shoals: Slavery to Success* would be greatly diminished.

Preface

This book was coauthored by Rickey Butch Walker and Huston Cobb Jr. We spent many hours together talking about the history and heritage of the Black folks who call the area of the Muscle Shoals of the Tennessee River of northwest Alabama home. Muscle Shoals refers to the areas of the Tennessee River from Decatur to the Mississippi state line and includes a series of six shoals including the Elk River Shoals, Big Muscle Shoals, Little Muscle Shoals, Colbert Shoals, Bee Tree Shoals, and Waterloo Shoals.

Mr. Cobb and many of his ancestors were residents of the Town Creek Triangle in present-day Colbert County, Alabama. The Town Creek Triangle is the land from Town Creek to the County Line Road in present-day Colbert County, Alabama. The Triangle was originally in Lawrence County, and it runs from the northeast corner of present-day Franklin County with the eastern boundary following Town Creek to the Tennessee River.

During the 1980s, Mr. Cobb interviewed several elderly Black folks who had spent most of their lives around the Town Creek Triangle of the Muscle Shoals area. Many of these people had ancestors who were slaves to the White cotton planters of northwest Alabama. The information found in those interviews and the historic events taking place from the days of slavery to the present are written about in this book.

I, Rickey Butch Walker, did several interviews with Mr. Cobb, and I toured with him the ancestral land of his youth. I wrote in detail about his life and the lives of his ancestors who lived in the Town Creek Triangle.

Rickey Butch Walker & Huston Cobb Jr.

In addition to Mr. Huston Cobb Jr., I did intensive interviews with two other Black gentlemen—Mr. Arthur Graves and Mr. Charlie Pointer. I also talked to other Black people about the lives and lifestyles of their folks who lived in the Muscle Shoals area of northwest Alabama.

I was very honored to coauthor and work with Mr. Huston Cobb Jr. on this book *Black Folktales of the Muscle Shoals: Slavery to Success*. Together we have recorded a small portion of the history, heritage, and culture of Black folks who lived along the Muscle Shoals.

Table of Contents

Introduction

Since Black folks at the Muscle Shoals in northwest Alabama were left out of the Alabama history books in most cases, it is difficult for the average person to understand the role the Black community played in the history and development of the Shoals area. Most people are not aware that Black folks were working and building the very foundation of the Muscle Shoals of northwest Alabama long before the first wealthy White cotton planters from Virginia and North Carolina were to arrive with large numbers of Black slaves starting in 1818.

It is impossible to examine the history of the Muscle Shoals area of the Tennessee River without looking at the Black folks who were here with the Chickasaw and Cherokee Indians. Not all Black folks were brought into northwest Alabama as slaves of White cotton planters, but they were here in the late 1700s as slaves of the Indian inhabitants.

Long before Alabama became a state, and even before the United States became a nation independent from the British, the Cherokee and Chickasaw Indians inhabited what is now northwest Alabama. Both tribes had legitimate claims that overlapped the lands of the Muscle Shoals of the Tennessee River Valley, and both Indian Nations were dealing in Black slaves during the late 1700s.

By 1782, James Logan Colbert of the Chickasaw Nation had accumulated and owned some 150 Black slaves that were supposedly stolen from French and Spanish

1

vessels navigating the Mississippi and Tennessee Rivers. Prior to his death on August 9, 1807, Chickamauga Cherokee Chief Doublehead and his White Irish brother-in-law, John Melton, owned some 100 Black slaves near Melton's Bluff on the Elk River Shoals in northwest Alabama.

At the time of the Turkey Town Treaty of 1816, both the Cherokee and Chickasaw had been farming cotton with the help of their Black slaves in the area of the Muscle Shoals on the Tennessee River. The Chickamauga Faction of Lower Cherokee were living and farming along the eastern portion of the Muscle Shoals, which included Elk River Shoals, Big Muscle Shoals, and Little Muscle Shoals. The Chickasaw were located along the western Shoals from Cane or Caney Creek in present-day Colbert County, Alabama, and into northeastern Mississippi. The western portion of the Shoals inhabited by the Chickasaws included the Colbert Shoals, Bee Tree Shoals, and Waterloo Shoals.

By the opening of Indian lands to settlement in 1818, many Blacks were already in the area and were slaves of the Indians. Much of the vast tracts of farmland along the Muscle Shoals of the Tennessee River were cleared and worked by Black folks, and many buildings across the area were constructed by slave labor, such as the historic state bank in Decatur, Alabama.

Today, several Black folks in the Muscle Shoals area of the Tennessee River of northwest Alabama are descendants of the slaves of the Chickasaw and Cherokee Indians. Many were removed with their Indian owners; however, a large number were sold and left in northwest Alabama. Of these Black people who were slaves to the Indians, some are actually of mixed Indian and Black ancestry, and they have reclaimed their Indian heritage through state-recognized tribal citizenship. Most of the Black-Indian students who were served in Lawrence County Schools' Indian Education Program had ancestors from the Melton's Bluff area of the Muscle Shoals.

There is more to read about the Black slaves of the Chickasaw and Cherokee Indians of the Muscle Shoals area of northwest Alabama. In the appendix in the back of this book, specific information can be found about who the Indian slave owners were and their relationship to the Muscle Shoals.

Slaves of White Planters

The White cotton planters bought the fertile lands near the Tennessee River for their cotton farming activities. Through the blood, sweat, and tears of their Black slaves, these early White planters passed their wealth and power to their White descendants.

Around 1807, the first of the White cotton planters with their Black slaves began arriving in Madison County of Mississippi Territory. On December 13, 1808, the northeast half of Madison County, including a portion of present-day Limestone County, became the first county in Mississippi Territory of present-day North Alabama. By 1809, White folks from Virginia and North Carolina, with their Black slaves, were pouring into the area of Madison County of Mississippi Territory along the Great South Trail leading south from Nashville, Tennessee.

According to the 1809 Census of Madison County, there were 322 Black slaves enumerated in the northeast half of what would become the present-day Madison County, Alabama. The northeast portion of Madison

3

County was created after the July 23, 1805, treaty with the Chickasaws and the January 7, 1806, Cotton Gin Treaty with the Cherokees.

After Doublehead and his followers signed the 1806 treaty, the Chickamauga faction of Lower Cherokees gave up their claims to the land north of the Tennessee River in northwest Alabama except Doublehead's Reserve to the west of Madison County. But in 1805, the Chickasaws just gave up their claims to the Madison County area of Mississippi Territory; therefore, they still maintained a claim on the land west of the original Madison County until the Turkey Town Treaty of 1816.

These 1805 and 1806 Indian treaties opened the lands of the original Madison County to White settlers, many of whom brought their Black slaves. The original western boundary of the county ran from the mouth of the Flint River on the Tennessee River about 45 degrees to the northwest to the Tennessee state line.

After the September 1816 Turkey Town Treaty, Indian people occupying the Muscle Shoals of the Tennessee River west of Madison County in Mississippi Territory of present-day northwest Alabama were removed. Those remaining Indians in northwest Alabama moved from the territory that makes up present-day Colbert, Franklin, Lauderdale, Lawrence, Limestone, Morgan, and the southwest half of present-day Madison Counties. Almost immediately, White cotton planters, mainly from Virginia and North Carolina, moved with their Black slaves into the Muscle Shoals area of the Tennessee Valley. These cotton planters purchased huge tracts of fertile Tennessee Valley soils ideal for growing cotton.

Trade Routes

With their free Black labor force, these wealthy planters and land barons used their slaves to enrich themselves and their families. The cotton and other farm products produced with slave labor were carried to New Orleans or Mobile by way of the Natchez Trace and Byler's Old Turnpike Road. From the gulf ports at Mobile and New Orleans, cotton and other plantation products were then sent to worldwide markets.

The Natchez Trace stretched 500 miles with 33 miles going across northwest Alabama. The Trace had its origin in Nashville, Tennessee, and ended in Natchez, Mississippi. The ancient path or overland route of Natchez Trace was used by the Indians centuries before the Black or White man arrived in northwest Alabama.

The Trace became a major return route from New Orleans to the Muscle Shoals area after the arrival of White planters with their Black slaves. From the antebellum period of the early 1800s to the Civil War, the Natchez Trace was used by commercial merchants of the cotton planters for many years as a major route north from New Orleans or Natchez to the Muscle Shoals and Nashville, Tennessee.

From the Muscle Shoals plantations of northwest Alabama, planter merchants and employees would navigate their flat/keel boats along the Tennessee River, to the Ohio River, and down the Mississippi River with cotton and other goods by Natchez, Mississippi, and on down to New Orleans, Louisiana. After all their plantation products and merchandise including the lumber in their watercrafts were sold in New Orleans, these boat operators would then come back up the Trace into the Shoals area of northwest Alabama or on to Nashville, Tennessee.

Byler's Old Turnpike Road was another major overland route for the transport of cotton and other farm produce of northwest Alabama plantations. The route ran south from the Muscle Shoals of the Tennessee River, passed through the Black Warrior Mountains that lay south from the Tennessee Divide, and on toward the Gulf of Mexico.

The Byler Road terminated at the head of navigation at the Falls of the Black Warrior River at present-day Northport, Alabama, then by water to Mobile. Other minor routes north and south were used to transport cotton and other farm products during the plantation days, but they were not as important as the Natchez Trace or Byler's Old Turnpike Road.

Black Labor

The Black slaves were the labor force of cotton planters in the Muscle Shoals area. Their slaves were not allowed to leave the land or plantation that they were living on without a pass from the White owner unless they were accompanied by him or his heirs.

Calling slaves by a given name was a common practice; therefore, it was not unusual for slaves to take their surname from the last name of the plantation owner or master. Today in the Muscle Shoals area, many Black families still use the surnames of the former White slave owners who used their ancestors to acquire wealth and large tracts of land.

Some Black slaves were probably born and died without ever leaving the cotton plantations where they were born and where they worked. Therefore, many of these Black families did not go far from the area where they and their immediate family were slaves until after the Civil War.

Black Folks picking cotton while overseer watches on horseback

According to the 1860 census records of the counties of northwest Alabama, Black slaves numbered some 40 to 50 percent of the population in most counties, with the White population being 50 to 60 percent of the population. However, shortly after the end of the Civil War, the numbers of Black folks in the Shoals area dropped to around 15 to 20 percent of the total population.

For example, according to the 1860 Lawrence County, Alabama, United States Census, the population included 7,173 Whites, 14 free Blacks, and 6,788 Black slaves. In 1860, 48.7 percent of the county was Black with 51.3 percent of the population being White. Years after the Civil War, the Black population of Lawrence County dropped to around 15 percent of the total population.

Since farm work was the predominate occupation in northwest Alabama in the years after the Civil War, many Black folks left the area to find work in the industrial factories of big cities and the northern portion of the United States. Many of the Black folks that remained in northwest Alabama have family members and relatives that still live in the northern industrial cities.

On the other hand, the descendants of Black slaves had to struggle for survival some 100 years after the end of the Civil War. Even after the war, Black women were many times subjected to the advances of wealthy and powerful White men, who often had children by their Black housemaids. Such was the case with some of the Black females who remained in the Muscle Shoals of the Tennessee River Valley. The Civil Rights Acts of the 1960s put Black folks on a more level status with the White families.

Today, the descendants of the slaves of these first White cotton planters make up the majority of the Black folks in the Muscle Shoals area of the Tennessee Valley of northwest Alabama. Most of the Black slave families of the Shoals area had descendants that survived and stayed in the homeland of their ancestors. Of the Black families that stayed near their birth site, many have deep family roots and some even purchased land on which their parents, grandparents, and great-grandparents were slaves.

Colbert County Tour

On January 4, 2013, I had the good fortune to meet a delightful eighty-seven-year-old Black gentleman by the name of Huston Cobb Jr. Huston had spent the majority of his life in the Town Creek Triangle of Colbert County, Alabama, where some of his ancestors were slaves to White planters of the area. After a two-hour interview of getting into the world of Huston Cobb, we took the first of a number of tours of his stomping grounds in the Triangle of the northeastern corner of Colbert County, Alabama.

We made stops at several cemeteries, as well as Bainbridge Loop, Second Street sites, Leighton, The Oaks Plantation Home, Mother Church/cemetery at The Oaks, LaGrange Mountain college site/cemetery, Jarman Plantation House, Shaw Plantation Home, Old Brick Church, Bethel Colbert Baptist Church, and the John Johnson Plantation House near old Cherokee village of Shoal Town at the mouth of Town Creek.

Mr. Huston Cobb Jr. gave a historical overview of the Black struggle and history of his homeland. In 1867, Colbert County was first established and was carved out of the northern half of Franklin County. The county was named in honor of George and Levi Colbert, who were Scots-Chickasaw mixed-bloods of the county. The original Colbert County boundary extended from the Mississippi state line east to the County Line Road, or what was known as Byler's Old Turnpike, and Doublehead's Trace.

In 1895, all of the land east of County Line Road, west of the stream called Town Creek, and north to the Tennessee River was annexed from Lawrence County into Colbert County, Alabama. The Lawrence County land annexed into Colbert County was known as the Town Creek Triangle.

The Triangle contained the most fertile, level, and excellent farmland for cotton production. Prior to the Civil War, the Triangle area attracted numerous large land-holding cotton planters from North Carolina and Virginia, who brought with them many Black slaves.

Among these wealthy slave-owning cotton planters were the families of King, Ricks, Madding, Hampton, Jarman, Preuit, Elliott, Foster, Johnson, Carter, Cobb, Saunders, Sherrod, and many others. Their Black slaves were the free labor force that planted and harvested the cash crop of cotton on many plantations scattered across the Muscle Shoals area of the Tennessee River.

According to Mr. Huston Cobb Jr., his folks were the slaves to some of the cotton planters mentioned above. Many of the Black ancestors of Mr. Cobb, coauthor of this book, lived most of their lives in the Town Creek Triangle of Colbert County.

Tuscumbia

Mr. Huston Cobb Jr. commented and wrote about the Colbert County towns, people, places, and history. Much of the following information is firsthand from his vast historical knowledge of his homeland along the Muscle Shoals.

East of George Colbert's Ferry along the Tennessee River at Natchez Trace, the first major town was known as Oka Kapassa (Ococoposa) or Cold Water. Around June 15, 1787, the Chickamauga Indian village of Coldwater was destroyed by General James Robertson and his forces from Nashville, Tennessee.

Present-day Tuscumbia Landing was near the site of the fight that occurred between Whites and Indians at Coldwater. An Indian trail known as the Coosa or Muscle Shoals Path circumvented the Muscle Shoals and ran south of the Tennessee River through the Moulton Valley connecting Ditto's Landing south of Huntsville to Tuscumbia Landing near Cold Water, the present-day Town of Tuscumbia.

When the first White settlers arrived in the area, the village was called Ococoposa, with its original Chickasaw name meaning cold water. Michael Dickson was one of the first White pioneers to come to the area by keel boat down the Tennessee River and settle in the town.

During 1820, Dickson purchased and owned many lots in the Town of Cold Water (present-day Tuscumbia) near the Big Spring, and he built one of the first houses in Tuscumbia.

By 1817, there were three houses, a mill, and a store near the Big Spring at present-day Tuscumbia. Along with Somerville and Courtland, Tuscumbia became one of the centers of the Cotton Kingdom on the south side of the Muscle Shoals area in northwest Alabama.

Several White planters who owned many Black slaves made their homes in the town with their vast cotton plantations scattered across the rich Tennessee River bottom lands. By the mid-1800s, the Tennessee River Valley of northwest Alabama from Huntsville westward to the Mississippi state line looked like one huge cotton plantation, with individual plantations butting against one another.

Prior to the construction of the railroad around the Muscle Shoals and the building of Wilson Dam, cotton planters, farmers, and their Black slaves could walk or drive a wagon across the Tennessee River at fords during low water periods. It was these crossings of the Muscle Shoals where the Indian name of "Chake Thlocko," meaning Great Crossing Place or Big Ford, was derived.

In 1820, the settlement was called Cold Water and became the first town in the area to be incorporated. In 1821, the name of the town was changed to Big Spring, and in 1822 the name was changed again to Tuscumbia, in honor of Chickasaw Chief Tuscumbia. At the spring in Tuscumbia, some 35 million gallons of water a day flow out of the limestone rock at Big Spring into Spring Creek, which flows into the Tennessee River on the west side of Tuscumbia Landing.

President of United States

Huston Cobb Jr. stated, "On Labor Day in 1980, Tuscumbia became an important site in a presidential campaign. President Jimmy Carter kicked off his bid for reelection as President of the United States at Tuscumbia, Alabama. I know of first in a lot of things, but I do not know of any other southern state where a United States President has kicked off his reelection campaign."

First Railroad

On June 23, 1832, the first railroad in Alabama and west of the Appalachians was opened and incorporated in Tuscumbia. Initially, the rail line ran from Tuscumbia to Tuscumbia Landing on the Tennessee River at the mouth of Spring Creek, about two miles northwest from town. This first railroad was used to transport cotton from the Town of Tuscumbia to the Tennessee River, where it could be loaded on keel boats headed to New Orleans and other profitable markets.

Mr. Huston Cobb Jr. said, "The opening of the railroad in Tuscumbia fired up the wealthy cotton planters in northwest Alabama. In June 1834, they eventually extended and completed the railroad from Tuscumbia to Decatur. The original railroad passed east from Tuscumbia through Leighton, Town Creek, Courtland, Hillsboro, and ended at Decatur."

After the railroad was extended some 42 miles east of Tuscumbia to Decatur, Alabama, Colonel Benjamin Sherrod became the first president of the railroad company. Sherrod, who was born in Halifax County, North Carolina, on January 16, 1777, was the nephew of Isaac Ricks and cousin of Abraham Ricks of The Oaks Plantation; Abraham was the son of Isaac.

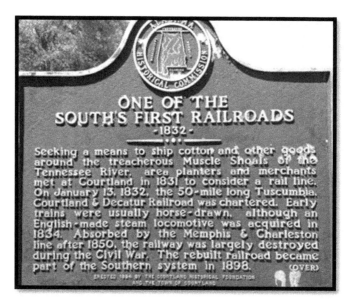

ONE OF THE
SOUTH'S FIRST RAILROADS
-1832-

Seeking a means to ship cotton and other goods around the treacherous Muscle Shoals of the Tennessee River, area planters and merchants met at Courtland in 1831 to consider a rail line. On January 13, 1832, the 50-mile long Tuscumbia, Courtland & Decatur Railroad was chartered. Early trains were usually horse-drawn, although an English-made steam locomotive was acquired in 1834. Absorbed by the Memphis & Charleston line after 1850, the railway was largely destroyed during the Civil War. The rebuilt railroad became part of the Southern system in 1898. (OVER)

ERECTED 1994 BY THE COURTLAND HISTORICAL FOUNDATION
AND THE TOWN OF COURTLAND

Colonel Sherrod was the wealthiest cotton planter involved in the Tuscumbia, Courtland, Decatur Railroad organization. He and his children owned a total of seven cotton plantations in the Muscle Shoals area of northwest Alabama and some 700 Black slaves. The plantations included Alamance in Lawrence County, Bear Creek five miles west of Tuscumbia, Chantilly near Highway 133 and Highway 20, Cotton Garden at Courtland, Hard Bargin at the Courtland airbase, Locust Grove in Colbert County, Pond Spring east of Courtland, and all of the island that became Patton Island at Florence.

Since the three upper shoals of the Muscle Shoals were impassable by boats transporting cotton during low water periods, the railroad was a priority for the large slave-holding plantation owners wanting to transport their cotton to the best markets. Therefore, many of the wealthy White plantation aristocrats became stockholders in this first railroad west of the Appalachians.

Colonel Benjamin Sherrod

The Tuscumbia-Courtland-Decatur Railroad enabled the wealthy cotton planters to get their products and goods to the New Orleans market when the Tennessee River was very low. Otherwise, they had to wait for high waters to get around the 37 miles of shoals which dropped in elevation some 134 feet between Decatur and Florence.

With their free Black labor force and the railroad, the White cotton planters in Muscle Shoals area continued to enrich themselves and their families. The hard, back-breaking work of Black slaves in the plantation cotton fields made the railroad investments of these plantation owners very profitable. The Black slaves were primarily responsible for making the White cotton planters and their extended families owners of vast tracts of land in the Tennessee Valley, which some of these families still own to this day.

Tuscumbia, Courtland, Decatur Railroad

Indian Removal

In addition, the Tuscumbia to Decatur Railroad was an asset to the United States Government during the Indian removal of the late 1830s. The railroad was used to transport Cherokee Indians around the Muscle Shoals to Tuscumbia Landing. At the landing, they would board steamers bound to areas west of the Mississippi River.

During the removal, many Cherokees in northeast Alabama and Chickasaws in northwest Alabama were being removed west. Some passed along the railroad from Decatur to Tuscumbia Landing on the Tennessee River. The rail line was a route around the Elk River Shoals, Big Muscle Shoals, and Little Muscle Shoals, which were barriers to navigation along the Tennessee River from Decatur to Tuscumbia.

The navigational water barriers along the Tennessee River at the shoals were created by vast layers of resistant chert (flint) rock. Therefore, the railroad was used to circumvent these natural obstacles that prevented water travel through the Muscle Shoals during low water periods. At Tuscumbia Landing, the Indians were placed on steamers and other watercraft to be transported west of the Mississippi River.

Again, the greed of the wealthy White cotton plantation owners helped provide for the ethnic cleansing of the Tennessee Valley of Indian people from 1816 through 1838. Indian removal of the Chickasaws and Cherokees made more of the former Indian territorial lands available to White cotton planters who were using Black slave labor.

LaGrange

At LaGrange, Mr. Huston Cobb Jr. gave me a history lesson on the first college in Alabama. He also told me about Abraham Ricks and The Oaks Plantation that Ricks owned at the northern base of LaGrange Mountain. The plantation of Ricks was in the valley just below and to the north of the college which was located on the mountain.

LaGrange College was east of Tuscumbia on top of LaGrange Mountain, some four miles southwest of Leighton. It was the first college chartered in Alabama with its doors opening on January 11, 1830, with two three-story brick buildings. The college was established by the Tennessee and Mississippi Methodist churches.

On January 19, 1830, LaGrange College became the first educational institution issued a charter by the Alabama Legislature with Reverend Robert Paine as the first president. A Cherokee and a Choctaw actually served on the Board of Trustees with General John Coffee, who surveyed the Indian lands that were taken in the Turkey Town Treaty of September 1816; however, Black folks were not included on the Board of Trustees of LaGrange College.

In 1830, Turner Saunders, a White cotton planter and owner of 50 Black slaves, was elected the first President of the Board of Trustees of LaGrange College. His home was supposedly designed by President Thomas Jefferson, and it had chains and shackles in the basement for Black slaves. The mansion still stands in Lawrence County just one mile east of Highway 101. Turner's son, James Edmonds Saunders, owned 145 Black slaves in 1860 at his Rocky Hill Castle.

Saunders, Hall, Goode Mansion

LaGrange became the finest center of learning in the South. It was used primarily for the education of White children of cotton planters coming into northwest Alabama from Virginia and North Carolina; however, Black children were not allowed to attend. At the same time these White children were attending school at LaGrange on top of the mountain, Black children of slave families were working in the cotton fields of Abraham Ricks and other cotton planters in the vast Tennessee Valley below the college.

In 1855, the college was beset by financial trouble; therefore, LaGrange College President Richard Rivers accepted an offer, a building, and financial support from Florence to move the college to Florence. The name was changed from LaGrange College to Wesleyan University because of legal problems. Later the name was change to Florence State Teachers College, and now it is called the University of North Alabama (UNA).

In 1857, the original property was taken over by the State of Alabama and became LaGrange College and Military Academy. In 1860, just prior to the Civil War, the name was changed to LaGrange Military Academy. The school was providing training for young White men in preparation of the Civil War and was known as the "West Point of the South." Many of these military cadets went on to become officers in the Confederate Army during the Civil War. Several of these Confederate military officers were accompanied into war with their Black slave servant.

On April 28, 1863, the LaGrange Military Academy and many of the White cotton planter mansions on the mountain and in the valley were burned by the Union forces of General Grenville M. Dodge. The 10th Missouri Calvary regiment of the United States Army under the command of Colonel Florence M. Cornyn was actually the unit that burned the school. Today, the old college site is used and maintained as a small Colbert County historical park.

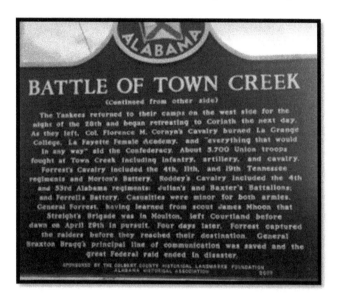

The Oaks Plantation

Mr. Huston Cobb Jr. directed us from Highway 157 to Colbert County Road 61, where we visited The Oaks Plantation of Abraham Ricks (son of Isaac Ricks), the home of Abe Sledge, Mother Church, and the Black cemetery. These four structures and features of the days of Black slavery are still visible today.

Abraham Ricks Sr. was the owner of The Oaks; he was born on October 10, 1791, in Halifax County, North Carolina. Abraham died at The Oaks in Colbert County,

Alabama, on December 23, 1852. The Ricks Family left North Carolina in 1818 with some 30 families, and Abraham brought his Black slaves to Alabama. Portions of the plantation were purchased during the United States government land sales of 1818.

The Oaks Plantation House
Rear view, 3/28/1935, Alex Bush
Library of Congress

The Ricks and King Families stopped briefly in Courtland, Alabama; the King Family moved to Leighton from Courtland in 1825. Ms. Bertie Ricks heard Mrs. Abraham Ricks, her grandmother, say that they moved to The Oaks on November 3, 1818.

A log cabin was already built at The Oaks by the Indians. Abraham Ricks added to the log cabin that was built by the Cherokees who occupied the area from the 1770 to 1816. The big part of the Ricks' house is in the same style as the little cabin, and they are attached. The Oaks home was located on the flat plain that lies along north edge of LaGrange Mountain in Colbert County, Alabama.

At The Oaks Plantation, Abraham Ricks accumulated some 300 Black slaves and 10,000 acres of land, which was part of the original land grant to Lemuel Sledge. Abraham Ricks was said to have treated his slaves very well. Many of the Black families of Colbert County are descendants of the approximately 300 slaves/servants of Abraham Ricks; these Black families were first listed in the census of 1870.

Old Slave Quarters–The Oaks
3/28/1935, Alex Bush
Library of Congress

George Ricks

According to Huston Cobb Jr., "Abraham Ricks was a very wealthy man that came with the first White settlers. He brought with him his Black slaves; one in particular was George Ricks."

Huston continued, "George Ricks established the first Black Church of Christ congregation in Alabama. He later established congregations in Mississippi and South Alabama. George rode to South Alabama and Corinth, Mississippi, on horseback.

"The little church that George Ricks established down on Wilson Lane is still standing; the first building was torn down. The building was used for a school up until about 1937. It continued to be used as a worshipping place for many years."

Mr. Huston Cobb said, "We are now in the process of restoring the building. We have put a chain link fence around the church. We plan to go out there once a year, or at least once a year to have service with all the congregations in the Valley participating. Different church congregations are all helping to restore the building.

"The Oaks home of Abraham Ricks was restored, and it is still called The Oaks. When Abraham Ricks arrived in the Valley of Colbert County, a portion of the house on the south side had already been built by the Cherokee Indians who lived here. This tells us that the Indians were not gone long before White settlers took over.

"Abraham Ricks was buried on LaGrange Mountain in the LaGrange Cemetery. It was said that it took 16 yokes of oxen to pull his tombstone up the mountain. The monument was imported from Italy."

Mother Church

From The Oaks Plantation House, Huston Cobb directed us to the first Black church in Alabama. Sometime around 1825, Abraham Ricks built his slaves a log church about a quarter mile south of his plantation home on the little dirt road that passed just east of the main house. The church was established as a Church of Christ; the church became known as the "Mother Church" or "Christian Home." Huston Cobb's family was members of the Church of Christ. Huston Cobb Jr. was an elder in the Westside Church of Christ in Leighton, Alabama.

According to Huston, "Abraham Ricks was a member of the Church of Christ, which was started by Alexander Campbell; Campbell broke from the Presbyterian Church in 1812, adopting baptism by immersion. Abraham Ricks wanted his Black slaves to go to church and be converted to Christianity; he allowed his slaves to be taught catechisms, which were Bible verses. My grandmother, Fannie Johnson Carter, taught her grandkids Bible verses in the same tradition of the catechisms taught to our slave ancestors."

One of the Black slave families of Abraham Ricks that attended the Mother Church was that of George Ricks. George Ricks was born in 1838 and died on Christmas day, December 25, 1908. Some claim that George Ricks was from Liberia, Africa; however, in 1808 slave trade from Africa was outlawed by the United States. Therefore, most of The Oaks slaves were probably descendants of those who had been in America prior to the stop of African slave trade.

Huston Cobb continued, "Parson George Ricks, a Black slave of Abraham Ricks, was the first preacher at the Mother Church. George helped set up other Black Churches of Christ in the area. During the time of George Ricks, all Black preachers were called parsons.

"Today, the third church building is still standing at the site of the original church. Material from the second church was used in the construction of the third building and included the original pews of the second church. The first church was a log building which was built about 1825. The second building was used until 1937 when it was replaced in 1940 with the building that is at the site today. The second building was torn down and replaced with a block building. Arthur Graves paid for putting the roof on the church that stands today.

"Fred Ricks, the grandson of Parson George, carried

on preaching at the Mother Church and later moved to Leighton, Alabama, some 10 miles north of The Oaks. All the Black churches in the area would go to the old original church one Sunday per year to have service."

Huston explained, "Several years ago, the great-great-granddaughter of Parson George, Lois Long, died in her 70s. Prior to her death, she and her husband revived the weekly services at the original church. Grant Ricks, Parson George's grandson, was the father of Nellie Mae Ricks Long, who was Lois Long's mother. Nellie Mae Ricks married Isaac Long, who had land on the Jackson Highway in Sheffield, Alabama."

After a short stop at the Mother Church, we went to the Black cemetery that was located just west of the church. After the Civil War, Parson George bought 320 acres of land around the church and gave one-half acre for the graveyard. The majority of the deceased Black folks buried in the cemetery are the descendants of the slaves of Abraham Ricks.

Abe Sledge Home

As we were making the tour of the old Black landmarks in northeast Colbert County, Huston Cobb Jr. showed us the home of Abe Sledge, who was a direct descendant of the slaves of The Oaks; Abraham Ricks owned the ancestors of Abe Sledge. The old home of Abe appears to be in good shape and looks to be occupied today.

Huston said, "The grandmother of Abe Sledge was Emma Ricks Sledge. She was known as Momma Emma and was the cook for the plantation. Momma Emma was born on November 7, 1866, and died on May 7, 1954. In 1930, the government interviewed Momma Emma through workers of the Library of Congress. Emma Sledge was a midwife that delivered both Black and White babies.

"Abe was born on The Oaks Plantation; Abe was born in the house where he died. Abe Sledge was a Black man; the Miles brothers repaired his old house which was located between The Oaks and the original Black Mother Church. The Sledge name came from a White family by the same name; Lemuel Sledge, a white man, owned half a section of land in the area."

Abe Sledge Home

The Black slaves with the surname of Sledge were the ancestors of Percy Tyrone Sledge. Percy was born in Leighton, Alabama, on November 25, 1940. During his life, he received the Rhythm and Blues Foundation's Career Achievement Award, and he was inducted into the Rock and Roll Hall of Fame in 2005. Percy was best known for his song "When a Man Loves a Woman." Percy Sledge died on April 14, 2015.

LaGrange Mountain Cemetery

Within a few miles southeast of The Oaks, Huston Cobb directed us to the LaGrange Mountain Cemetery where Abraham Ricks Sr. was buried in December 1852. LaGrange is a French word that means "The Place." The mountaintop cemetery was just south of LaGrange College.

By far, the largest monument of Italian marble in the cemetery was that of Abraham Ricks, Sr. He was probably the largest land and slave owner of the LaGrange Mountain area, and his burial site represents his great wealth.

Abraham Ricks Tombstone

Leighton

Another stop on the tour with Mr. Huston Cobb Jr. was the little town of present-day Leighton. He told us that the settlement was originally known as Jeffrey's Crossroads, which was a few miles south of Second Street in present-day Colbert County.

By 1770, the area of Jeffrey's Crossroads was claimed by the Chickamauga faction of the Lower Cherokees. However, the area was actually recognized by the United States government as Chickasaw land by the Chickasaw Boundary Treaty of January 10, 1786.

The original Town of Jeffrey's Crossroads was located at the junction of Doublehead's Trace (Byler Road) and the Upper River Road (Tuscumbia-Courtland Stage Road).

The town was one of the early mixed settlements of Celtic Indian people established around 1808. This mixed Cherokee and Scots Irish settlement was one of many that were in North Alabama prior to the Indian removal from the area in 1816.

Many members of the Jeffrey Family were mixed blood Celtic Indians of Scots Irish and Cherokee ancestry. Today, descendants of the original Jeffrey surname still reside in the Muscle Shoals area. Some are state-recognized Indians and are tribal citizens of the Echota Cherokee Tribe of Alabama.

The territory around Leighton remained Indian land until the Turkey Town Treaty of 1816; the treaty was ratified by congress in July 1817. Shortly after the treaty, White cotton planters with their Black slaves flooded the area and began buying up the land during the 1818 federal lands sales.

Mr. Cobb said, "Originally, the west half of Leighton was in Franklin County from 1818 until February 6, 1867; in 1867, the west half became Colbert County. The east half of Leighton was in Lawrence County. In 1895, the east half was annexed from Lawrence County into Colbert County."

Gregg Tavern

As early as 1810, the Gregg Tavern at Jeffrey's Crossroads served the needs of travelers in northwest Alabama. In 1820, Gregg Tavern was selected as a tollbooth on Byler's Old Turnpike that is known today as the County Line Road.

Mr. Huston Cobb Jr. stated, "In 1912, the old Gregg Tavern was moved one block west to its present location in Leighton. The tavern building was pulled by a horse using pine logs as rollers to move it. I was told by Robert Layton Jr. that his grandfather, Mr. Clyde King, made a bet that his horse could pull the house, and of course he won. The side of the house facing Highway 20 is the back of the house. I do not suppose they trusted the horse to try to turn the house around, so they left it backwards."

Huston stated, "After Claude King moved the small stagecoach stop building west of the intersection of County Line Road and old Highway 20, he built a fine brick home; both old houses are still standing. Today, about one block west of the traffic light in Leighton, Gregg Tavern still stands as the oldest house in Leighton. The tavern was originally at the crossroads one block to the east."

On our tour through Leighton, Huston Cobb pointed out the Westside Church of Christ that he attended; he also pointed out houses that were owned by Claude King. The King Family came to the area with Abraham Ricks of The Oaks and some 30 other families.

29

Leigh Family

About 1823, the William Leigh Family came to Alabama from Amelia County, Virginia, and purchased large tracts of land around the Town of Jeffrey's Crossroads.

After the family of William moved to the town, it was named in honor of the William Leigh Family and became known as Leighton, Alabama. William Leigh was head of an early White cotton planter family that moved with several Black slaves to the settlement.

According to the 1830 census, William Leigh owned 38 Black slaves, and Robert H. Leigh owned 21 Black slaves. Hershel Leigh, a descendant of the Leigh Family from the Town of Leighton, married Annie Frances Alexander, a descendent of the Alexander Plantation just southeast of Moulton.

Leighton Training School

During the historical tour with Mr. Cobb, we visited the remains of his boyhood school. The school was located on the west side of Leighton, and it was abandoned many years ago. The facility was for Black children and was known as the Leighton Training School; however, it was just about deteriorated.

Huston Cobb Jr. said, "After desegregation, the Leighton Training School was abandoned because it was in a predominately Black neighborhood in the Town of Leighton." The school eventually collapsed with only the front brick walls still standing.

Leighton Training School

Byler's Old Turnpike Road

On our tour of Colbert County, Mr. Huston Cobb Jr. directed us to the Bainbridge Loop of Byler's Old Turnpike. Originally, the Loop was a portion of Doublehead's Trace leading south from the crossing of the Tennessee River at Bainbridge. The Bainbridge Loop portion is still as it was many years ago except that it is paved, but you can clearly see the old sunken road of years gone by.

The Byler's Old Turnpike Road was the first highway approved by the Alabama state legislature in Huntsville on December 16, 1819, only two days after statehood when Alabama was admitted into the Union. The Byler Road ran south from Jackson's Military Road Bridge over Shoals Creek near the home of Samuel Craig in Lauderdale County to Northport, Alabama, at the falls of the Black Warrior River.

John Byler and Associates were authorized by the state of Alabama to build the turnpike. According to state legislation, the road was to begin at Samuel Craig's house on the south side Jackson's Military Road Bridge crossing Shoals Creek in Lauderdale County; however, there was a portion of the Byler Road in Lauderdale County that was never constructed.

From the Military Road, now known as Jackson Highway or Highway 43 in Lauderdale County, Byler's Old Turnpike Road was to proceed southwest across Lauderdale County. The old road crossed the Muscle Shoals of the Tennessee River from Lauderdale County to the Town of Bainbridge located in present-day Colbert County.

According to Mr. Cobb, "Bainbridge

Jackson's Old Military Road-bridge abutment in Shoals Creek

32

was known to some as Cunningham Valley. The road passed by Hawkins Creek Church, through Bainbridge Loop, and across Second Street Road, going southeast until it intercepted the county lines of then Franklin and Lawrence Counties.

"The Byler Road passed by the old Buck Boone (Beth Boose) house, which was an old slave house; it was owned by a Black man known as Boone (Boose) who owned 320 acres of land. The Cunningham Valley Road, or Byler's Old Turnpike Road, intersected the county line of then Franklin and Lawrence where Jarman Lane began. Jarman Lane, named after the Amos Jarman Plantation, was actually an extension of Avalon Avenue in the Town of Muscle Shoals, Alabama. Initially, Avalon Avenue ran straight through the airport to the west beginning of Jarman Lane at the county line."

In 1837, Amos Jarman, a cotton planter from Jones County, North Carolina, was appointed the commissioner and overseer of Byler's Old Turnpike. The Byler's Old Turnpike Road continued from Jarman Lane through Leighton or Jeffrey's Crossroads, then passed through the Black Warrior Mountains to the southwest, then to the Falls of the Black Warrior River, or Tuscaloosa River, at Northport, Alabama. Tuscaloosa is a Creek Indian word that means Black Warrior; Tusca means warrior, and Loosa means black.

According to the state law, Byler's Old Turnpike was to be twelve feet wide and cleared of all stumps. Low places were to be covered or raised, and all streams bridged. In 1828, the road became a United States mail route, and in 1830, it became a regular stagecoach route.

Although the Byler Road never gained the same fame as the Natchez Trace, it was the main link between the Muscle Shoals area at Bainbridge and the head of the navigation at the Falls of the Black Warrior River at Northport, Alabama, until 1850. From Northport, water navigation was utilized to get cotton and other farm goods to ports in Mobile. Thus, the Byler's Old Turnpike road system was part of a Mobile-to-Nashville Trace which connected Nashville, Tennessee, to the ocean port at Mobile, Alabama.

Spring Hill Plantation

As we were touring the ancestral stomping grounds of Huston's family, he pointed out the home of a White cotton planter by the name of Bernard McKiernan, who owned Spring Hill Plantation. The old plantation home site was just west of McKiernan Creek and north of the River Road in present-day Colbert County. Today, the old hilltop home place still has a stand of the old red cedar trees that mark the location of the original plantation house.

McKiernan Creek is about one mile west of the present-day crossroads of the River Road and County Line Road at Ford City in Colbert County, Alabama. Later, one of the White McKiernan girls married a Dunagan man from Huntsville. After their marriage, the couple lived for a while near the creek on the Spring Hill Plantation; therefore, the area of McKiernan Creek became known as Dunagan Slough.

Huston Cobb Jr. said, "My mother-in-law, Mary Long, learned to swim in McKiernan Creek." Today, I, Rickey Butch Walker, have a home on McKiernan Creek of Wilson Lake about one mile north of the River Road. My river house is on land of the original Spring Hill Plantation.

Bernard McKiernan

The Spring Hill Plantation of Bernard McKiernan was not far west of Huston's boyhood home. The creek of the drainage area around Ford City in Colbert County was named in honor of Bernard McKiernan, who owned the vast cotton plantation. According to the slave census of 1850, Bernard McKiernan owned 92 Black slaves.

Bernard McKiernan would rent his slaves out to other farmers for a small fee. On a nearby plantation of Levi Guest, there was a slave by the name of Peter, and his family was slaves of Bernard. Peter bought his freedom from Guest, and he went north by way of the Underground Railroad. In the north, he made enough money to pay a White man to get boat and come back to Colbert County to steal his family from Bernard McKiernan and bring them north. The White man who was paid by the former slave got caught while traveling the Ohio River near Paducah, Kentucky. The White man tried to escape by jumping to another boat and drowned. The Black slaves were returned to Bernard Mckiernan. Eventually, Peter earned $5,000 to pay for the freedom of his family.

Charles McKiernan

Charles McKiernan was the son of Bernard. Huston Cobb told a story that had been passed down through several generations of Black folks in the area. He said, "Charlie McKiernan punished one of his Black slaves by putting a saddle on the man and riding him until he died. Charlie McKiernan also made some of his slaves eat watermelons rind and all because he thought they had stolen some of his melons."

According to the 1870 census of South Florence Post Office, Alabama, Charles McKiernan was listed as the head of the household which contained four Blacks and one Mulatto boy as follows: 54/54, McKiernan, Charles, age 54, male, White, farmer, born in TN; Rebecca, age 40, female, White, keeping house, born in TN; Charles, age 21, male, White, born in AL; Mary, age 14, female, White, at home, born in AL; Jacobsen, Mary, age 53, female, White, from Sweeden; Bailey, Parmelia, age 40, female, White, born in AL; Levi A. Bailey, age 20, male, White, farm laborer, born in AL; John, age 17, male, White, AL; Patrek, Josephine, age 22, female, Black, cook, born in AL; Stephen, age two, male, Black, born in AL; McKiendan, Harriet, age 18, female, Black, milk maid, born in AL; Laura, age two, female, Black, born in AL; Sambo, age 5/12, male, Mulatto, born in AL; McKiernan is Charles B. McKiernan. In the 1880 census, Levi A. Bailey was listed as head of household, with his mother and sister.

According to the 1870 census of Colbert County, some 30 Black and Mulatto folks with the last name McKiernan are listed as living in the area of South Florence Post Office. These former McKiernan slaves took the last name of their master.

Dr. Wayne Stanley

While on our historic tour of the Town Creek Triangle with Mr. Huston Cobb Jr., we stopped by the beautiful home of a Black doctor by the name of Wayne Stanley. According to Huston Cobb Jr., "My brother, Ernest Cobb, married Helen Stanley who was the great-great-granddaughter of former slave Lila Vinson King. Helen was the daughter of O. C. Stanley and Elsie King. Helen Stanley had a brother, Henry Leon Stanley, who married Helen Louise Gadd. Henry and Helen Stanley had a son who is Doctor Wayne Stanley."

Huston continued, "Doctor Wayne Stanley is known as one of the best medical doctors in the northwest Alabama area. He is a descendant of a former slave and former slave owner. He was the grandson of O. C. Stanley, and his grandmother was Elsie King Stanley, a descendant of Black slaves

Elsie King Stanley

and White slave owners. Elsie was the Mulatto daughter of Lou Bell (Momma Bell) King and granddaughter of Lila Vinson King. Elsie was thought to be the daughter of one of the White King Family slave owners." The King Family of Colbert County owned some 300 Black slaves.

Today, Dr. Wayne Stanley has a beautiful hilltop mansion with a big metal gate at the entrance of his drive just south of Second Street. His huge spacious home sits on a hill with a magnificent view of the former land that his ancestors worked as slaves.

White Stanley Family

The White Stanley Family came into the area during the 1818 federal sales of Indian lands taken by government in September 1816 by the Turkey Town Treaty. The Stanley Family with their Black slaves, along with several other wealthy White slave owners, came from North Carolina and Virginia to the Tennessee Valley seeking vast tracts of fertile cotton ground.

By the time of the 1820 Census of Lawrence County, Alabama, Syrus Stanley was listed as having five Black slaves. His family consisted of one White male over 21 years of age, three White males under 21 years of age, one female over 21 years of age, and four females under 21 years of age.

In the 1830 Census of Lawrence County, Alabama, Henry Stanley was listed as a White male between 50 and 60. In his household, the following individuals were identified: one White male between 20 and 30; one White male between 10 and 15; two White males under five; one White female between 20 and 30; and one White female under five.

Also in 1830, Nathaniel Stanley was listed as a White between 40 and 50. In his household, the following individuals were identified: one White male between 20 and 30; one White male between 15 and 20; one White male between 10 and 15; two White males between five and 10; and one White male under five. In addition, three White females were listed in Nathaniel Stanley's family, with one between 40 and 50, one between 20 and 30, and one between 10 and 15.

The members of the Stanley Family were owners of Black slaves. According to the 1850 slave census of Lawrence County, Andrew Stanley had six slaves, Joseph Stanley had 55 slaves, and Edward Stanley had 34 slaves. By the 1860 census, Andrew Stanley owned 11 black slaves and J. H. and E. R. Stanley owned 42 slaves. Many of the

Black folks who were descendants of the slaves of the Stanley Family took Stanley as their last name.

According to the 1850 census, Joseph H. Stanley was 38 years old and from North Carolina, and his wife Mariah L. was 30 years old and from Virginia. Also living in the household of Joseph H. Stanley were the following: Joseph H. Stanley Jr., age 10, born in Alabama; Thomas E., age five, born in Alabama; Hannah Kemper, age 17, born in Alabama; and John Green, age 70, from North Carolina. John was probably the father of Mariah.

In the 1850 census, Edward R. Stanley was listed as being age 26 and born in Alabama, Mary J. was age 26 and born in Virginia, Edward R. Jr. was age four and born in Alabama, and Margaret Hill was age 70 and born in Virginia. Margaret Hill was probably the grandmother to either Edward or Mary. Edward and Joseph were probably brothers.

Stanley Home–August 1963

The old Stanley home was built by either Nathaniel or Andrew Hopkins Stanley. The following are tombstone records of the old Stanley Cemetery near Brick-Hatton Community in northeastern Colbert County, Alabama, which was surveyed by Joseph L. Stanley in April 1965 and contributed by Jackie Stone on June 27, 2006. There are only 18 graves in the old cemetery, and the spelling and abbreviations are as shown on the tombstones.

1. Emma I. Daughter of A. J. and E. E. Stanly, March 5, 1855–July 12, 1855.

2. Katie E. Dau. of J. and S. E. Trousdale, March 8, 1867–July 28, 1870. (Other non-Stanley names may have been neighbors.)

3. William J. Stanly, June 21, 1850–May 30, 1872.

4. Edward R. Stanley, April 24, 1824–Jan 17, 1862.

5. Edward S. Stanly son of E. R. and M. J. Stanly, Dec. 19, 1860–Aug. 28, 1871.

6. Andrew H. Stanly son of E. R. and M. J. Stanly, Dec. 9, 1856–June 23, 1857.

7. John W. Stanly son of E. R. and M. J. Stanly, July 1, 1851–Sept 26, 1855.

8. Ellen wife of Nathaniel Stanly, Born Oct 30, 1780–Died June 28, 1843.

9. Franklin N. Stanly son of A. H. and M. A. Stanly, Born July 24, 1843–Died Sept 8, 1846.

10. A child (not legible), Born June 16, 18?–Died June 27, 1852.

11. Andrew H. Stanley, June 8, 1822–July 10, 1888.

12. Sara Mays, Born Amhurst Co, Va, May 20, 1799–Dec. 19, 1887. (Sara Mays was the mother of Martha A. Stanley.)

13. Dr. William A. Stanley, Born July 22, 1846–Died Aug. 20, 1886.

14. Eliz H. Carter, wife of J. A. Letsinger, Born Apr. 15, 1841–Jan 26, 1900. (Other non-Stanley names may have been neighbors.)

15. Martha A. Stanly, wife of A. H. Stanly, Born in Va, Dec 1?, 1821–Oct. 28, 1880.

16. Maria A., dau of A. J. and E. E. Stanly, July 21, 1853–July 21, 1854.

17. Maria L. wife of Joseph H. Stanly, 1819–Dec. 23.

18. Joseph Hopkins Stanley sen, May 4, 1812–Aug. 23, 1852.

Jarman Plantation

During our tour of his ancestral land in northeastern Colbert County, Huston Cobb Jr. guided us to the Jarman Plantation Home located in the Town Creek Triangle. The Amos Jarman place was a landmark during the life of Huston Cobb Jr., and the cotton plantation was located in the area that he called home. Many of the Black neighbors of Huston were descendants of the slaves of the Jarman Family.

In 1820, Amos Jarman built a large two-story brick house in the Brick Community about one mile east of Underwood Crossing and one-half mile north of Second Street in Colbert County, Alabama. The home is a beautiful brick house that is on the flat plain between the River Road and Second Street.

Amos Jarman Plantation Home

The Jarman Plantation was owned by Amos Jarman who was born on November 13, 1789, and died on December 14, 1861. His wife was Mary, who was born in 1790.

In the 1850 census, Amos and Mary were listed as 60 years old. They were living in the household with James C. Vincent, age 32 from Virginia, William H. Jarman, age 26 from Alabama, and D.F., who was a 23-year-old male. According to the 1850 Census of Lawrence County, Alabama, Amos Jarman owned 50 Black slaves.

According to the 1860 Census of Lawrence County, Alabama, Amos Jarman was 70 years old and a cotton planter from North Carolina. In his household at the time, Mary was listed as 70 years old from North Carolina, George

Amos Jarman and Mary Green Jarman

W. was a 32-year-old teacher born in Alabama, and Neppie was a 30-year-old female from Tennessee.

On December 14, 1861, Amos Jarman died at his Brick Community residence. However, his heirs continued to live in the house for many years. The original plantation house of Amos Jarman is still standing, occupied, and in good condition.

According to Huston Cobb Jr., "The Jarman Family eventually moved to Nashville, Tennessee, and founded the Jarman Shoe Company. So when you bought Jarman Shoes, you knew that the people who founded the company were from the Town Creek Triangle of Colbert County, Alabama. Jarman Shoes eventually merged with another company, and the Jarman Shoe line is no longer available."

Huston Cobb Jr. said, "My brother Leo Cobb married Nazarene Jarman, who was a descendant of the former slave Lila Vinson King. Nazarene was born on Jarman Lane and was one of 12 siblings. She was a descendant of the White King Family and the Black slaves of the Jarman Family. Two of Nazarene's aunts married descendants of the mixed-blood Black and White Spangler and Mullins Family."

Jarman Lane is south of Second Street and the Jarman Plantation Home. The lane is a blacktopped county highway that ends to the west on the County Line Road. Jarman Lane is where some of the slave descendants of Amos Jarman live today. Probably many of the Black folks in the area of present-day northeastern Colbert County, Alabama, are descendants of the Jarman Plantation slaves.

Brick Community

Some of the ancestors of Huston Cobb Jr. lived in the Brick Community, which was reported in some census records as Brickville. We toured the early Brick Community, and Mr. Cobb discussed the history of the area

Mr. Huston Cobb Jr. said, "The area was called Brick because of four very early 1800s buildings in the area were built with bricks made by Black slaves. The four buildings were the Jarman House, John Johnson House, Abernathy House, and Brick Church."

The original log church at Brick was completed in September 1820 and burned to the ground in 1824. Black slaves of the church members made the bricks for construction of the new church, which was built just southwest of Shegog Creek and Spring.

The Shegog Family was probably the origin of the name of the spring and creek. The 1860 Census of Lawrence County, Alabama, lists the following: George Shegog, age 35, Ireland, physician; Mariah, female, age 28; John S., age four; and George H., age one.

During the tour with Huston Cobb Jr., we stopped at the Old Brick Presbyterian Church which was one of the original White churches in Colbert County. Huston said, "The Jarman Family supposedly attended the church with their Black slaves. The church had a balcony at the back of the building that was used as the Black slave gallery for those slaves who attended the services, because they were not allowed to sit with the White folks."

THE OLD BRICK
PRESBYTERIAN CHURCH
1820

Old Brick Church began in 1820 as the Mt. Pleasant Cumberland Presbyterian Church and met in a frame building which burned in 1824. The present building has undergone few changes since its construction in 1828 when the congregation was officially chartered. In 1906 the congregation joined with what became the United Presbyterian Church in the U.S.A. It officially took its present name in 1961. In 1983 Old Brick became a part of the Presbyterian Church (U.S.A.). Sunday services have been conducted regularly since 1820, except during the Civil War.

The building bricks used in construction of the homes and church at Brick were made from clay that was dug and fired in pits by the slaves. The brick-making site and activities used in making the bricks were in close proximity to the Old Brick Presbyterian Church. The slave bricks were fired, hardened, and still form the walls of the church that was completed on October 8, 1828.

The church members were not allowed to work their slaves on Sundays. During the Civil War, there were no services at the church; supposedly, Confederate General John Bell Hood used Old Brick Church as his headquarters. The name of the church was eventually changed from Mount Pleasant to Old Brick.

Bethel Colbert Baptist Church

We visited Bethel Colbert Missionary Baptist Church where Huston Cobb Jr. attended when he was a young boy. Huston was a member of the church for 22 years.

Huston said, "Bethel Colbert Missionary Baptist Church had a little building to store a mule-drawn hearse that the church owned. If someone died, the church provided the hearse to carry the deceased to the cemetery for burial."

The Bethel Colbert Church property was bought on May 2, 1911, for the Black folks in the area and originally belonged to the slave-owning family of Baldy Shaw. Baldy was born about 1820, and he owned land from Sixth Street to Second Street in Colbert County. The road that runs past the Shaw Farm and the old home of Huston Cobb Jr. is called Shaw Road. J. C. Shaw deeded one and three-quarter acres of his property on Second Street to the family of Huston Cobb Jr. for the Black church.

Huston Cobb Jr. still has a copy of the deed for the Bethel Colbert Baptist Church where he attended church in his youth. The deed is as follows:

"Act of said corporation. Given under my hand this 2 day of May 1911. John E. Delony, Jr., Notary Public. State of Alabama. I, Oscar G. Simpson, Judge of Probate in and for said State and County, Colbert County. Know all men by these presents, That I, J. C. Shaw, an unmarried man, for and in consideration of One Dollar to me in hand paid the receipt whereof is hereby acknowledged, do hereby grant, bargain, sell, release, quit claim and convey unto Tom Cobb, Cole Johnson, Ed Hill, Alex Stanley and Tom Carter as Trustees and Deacons of the Bethel Colbert

46

Baptist Church (Colored) of Colbert County, Alabama, and their successors in office, the following described real estate lying and being in Colbert County, Alabama, and more particularly described as follows: Commencing at the N. W. corner of Section 35, thence running South 472-1/2 feet to a stake, thence East 139-1/2 feet; thence North 472-1/2 feet to a stake, thence West 139-1/2 to a stake in Section 35, Township 3, Range 9, in said Colbert County, Alabama containing 1.3/4 acres. To have and hold unto the said Tom Cobb, Cole Johnson, Ed Hill, Alex Stanley and Tom Carter as Trustees and Deacons of the said Bethel Church (Colored) and their successors in office forever. Witness my hand and seal on this the 4th day of May, 1911. J. C. Shaw (Seal)

State of Alabama, Colbert County, I, John R. Ayers, a Notary Public in and for said County in said state hereby certify that J. C. Shaw whose name is signed to the foregoing conveyance, who is known to me, acknowledged before me on this day that being informed of the contents of the conveyance, he executed the same voluntarily on the day the same bears name. Given under my hand this the 4th day of May, 1911, John R. Ayers, Notary Public.

State of Alabama, Colbert County, I, Oscar G. Simpson, Judge of Probate in and for said State and County, hereby certify that the foregoing conveyance was filed in this office for record on the 4th day of May, 1911, and recorded in Deed Record Vol. 15, page this 4th Day of May, 1911. Oscar R. Simpson, Judge of Probate."

Tom Cobb, Cole Johnson, and Tom Carter were great uncles of Huston Cobb Jr. They helped build and organize the Black church in the early 1900s for the descendants of former slaves that remained in the area after the Civil War.

The Houston Cobb Sr. Family attended Bethel Colbert Baptist Church when Huston Jr. was a small child. Huston was a member and attended the church until he was 32 years old.

Huston continued, "After people went to the mourner's bench to get their religion, they would later be baptized thinking their sins had already been forgiven; so the consensus was that you were saved when you got your religion. Then after many years, I found out that baptism was for the remission of sins; then the question was why you got the religion."

Huston disagreed with the Baptists, and he realized that the Church of Christ teaches baptism was the way of salvation. Therefore, because of his Biblical realizations, Huston started going to the Church of Christ, which was more in line with his beliefs. When Huston left the Baptist church, a total of 16 other members of the Baptist congregation left with him. The members changing to the Church of Christ included his daddy and mother, Houston Sr. and Nazareth Cobb. Since his family moved their membership to the Westside Church of Christ in Leighton, Alabama, Huston has been a member of the church over 60 years.

Shaw Plantation

We toured the Shaw cotton plantation home. We also went to the cemetery where Baldy Shaw and his wife were buried. The Shaw farm was not far from where Huston Cobb Jr. grew to manhood in the Town Creek Triangle.

Shaw Plantation House

Houston Sr. and his boys farmed the land where Huston Jr. lived for many years near the corner of Second Street and Shaw Road, named after the White Shaw Family. After the Cobb Family gathered their cotton crops, Houston Sr. and his family would hire out to pick cotton on the old Baldy Shaw Farm. At the time, the Tidwell Family was renting and planting cotton on the former Shaw slave owner's property. Huston and his family picked cotton on the Shaw Plantation and would be paid fifty to seventy-five cents per one hundred pounds of cotton they picked.

According to the 1850 Census of Lawrence County, Alabama, Baldy Shaw was listed as being 30 years old from North Carolina, but according to his tombstone, he would have been 56 years old in 1850. His tombstone record indicates he was born in 1794 and was 59 years old at his death. In the 1830 census, Baldy was listed as being between 30 and 40 years old and in 1840 census, Baldy Shaw was listed as being between 40 and 50 years old, which was in line with his tombstone record.

According to the 1850 slave census, Baldy Shaw owned 15 Black slaves; by 1860, he owned 24 Black slaves that would be divided among two heirs. In the 1850 census, his family was listed as Lemenda, age 43, from Kentucky; William H., age 19, Alabama; Martha F., age 17; Lemenda, age 15; Jessee C., age five; and Henry, age 48, from North Carolina.

Many of the Shaw Family were buried in the Shaw Cemetery, which is on Sixth Street about one-half mile west of where the Shaw Road dead ends on Sixth Street. The Shaw Plantation home is between Second Street and Sixth Street and some two miles south from Second Street. The north end of Shaw Road is Second Street and the south end is Sixth Street.

Slave Owner Families

During his lifetime, Huston Cobb Jr. heard many in his family tell of the White slave owners that lived in the area of his boyhood home. Quite often, Huston's folks had dealings with the former slave-holding families. Prior to the Civil War, many of his kinfolks were owned by the various White cotton plantation families.

During my tours and interviews with Mr. Huston Cobb Jr., he mentioned some White slave owners that were in his neighborhood. Below are a few of the White cotton plantation owners that he recalled that influenced the area where he and his family spent the majority of their lives.

Edward Pearsall

The family of Edward Pearsall owned large tracts of land. In the 1850 Census of Franklin County, Edward Pearsall owned 62 Black slaves.

The Pearsall Family was probably one of the roughly 30 original families that came to northwest Alabama with Abraham Ricks. The Pearsall place was on Highway 133 and the old airport.

Fennel Family

The Fennel Family also came to the area with Abraham Ricks of The Oaks Plantation. The Fennels owned tracts of cotton land that were scattered all over Colbert, Lawrence, and Morgan Counties.

According to the 1860 Census of Lawrence and Morgan Counties, the Fennel Family owned 132 Black slaves. After the Civil War, five of the Fennel brothers owned Fennel cotton gin and Fennel Brothers store.

Colonel John Townsend Abernathy

Huston Cobb Jr. said, "Colonel John Townsend Abernathy, a cotton planter from Virginia, had one of first brick houses in the northeast portion of Colbert County, Alabama. The Abernathy home was located on Second Street just west of the County Line Road."

Remains of the brick Abernathy House
February 1959

According to the 1860 census records of Franklin and Lawrence Counties, John T. Abernathy owned 136 Black slaves. James William Abernathy and Robert Towns Abernathy, two of the sons of John, owned 51 Black slaves. Many of the Black folks in northwest Alabama are descendants of the Abernathy slaves.

John T. Abernathy died on July 27, 1869, and he was buried at the Abernathy Cemetery near Leighton. According to Huston Cobb Jr., "Eventually, the family of John T. Abernathy sold his home and 320 acres of land to one of their former Black slaves by the name of Beef Boose Abernathy."

Samuel Hennigan

Samuel S. Hennigan Sr. was from Mecklenburg County, North Carolina; his wife was Nancy. Nancy Hennigan was listed in the 1820 Census of Lawrence County, Alabama, as being 76 years old and from Virginia.

At the time of the 1820 census, Nancy Hennigan was living in the household of Hall Jarman, age 36, from North Carolina. Also living in the house of Hall Jarman was Harriet, age 52 from New York; Permelia age 24 from Alabama; Sarah E., age 17; and Jesse Nelms, age 21, from Alabama.

Hall Jarman was the son of Amos Jarman. In the 1850 Lawrence County Census, Hall Jarman owned 15 Black slaves.

Samuel Stuart Hennigan Jr. bought the John H. Johnson home place, which was known as The Green Onion Plantation. According to the 1860 Lawrence County, Alabama, Census, Samuel S. Hennigan Jr. owned 56 Black slaves.

Rosenwald Schools

During the tour with Huston Cobb Jr., he pointed to locations of a few local schools in Colbert County that were built for Black children. The schools were part of a project of a Jewish man, Julius Rosenwald   (August 12, 1862– January 6, 1932). Rosenwald was part-owner and leader of Sears, Roebuck and Company. Paul J. Sachs, senior partner of Goldman Sachs, introduced Rosenwald to Black educator Booker T. Washington, who in 1912 served on the Board of Directors of Tuskegee Institute in Alabama.

Booker T. Washington asked Rosenwald to help poor Black children get an adequate education. Initially, Rosenwald provided money to construct six schools in rural Alabama that were opened between 1913 and 1914. Starting in 1917, the Rosenwald Fund constructed some 5,800 schools and educational facilities for poor children across the South.

Julius Rosenwald

Huston Cobb Jr. was familiar with three of the Rosenwald schools that were built for Black children and one for White children in Colbert County, Alabama:

1. One Rosenwald school was located at Mount Pleasant on the County Line Road.

2. Another Rosenwald school was located at the south end of Ford Road near Wise (previously Reynolds) and was called Pond Creek or Mt. Olivia.

3. Another Rosenwald school was between Barton and Cherokee.

4. A Rosenwald school for White students was on Mt. Stanley Road and was called Midway School.

Houston Cobb Sr.

According to Huston Cobb Jr., on October 4, 1902, Houston Cobb Sr. was born in the Town Creek Triangle on the north side of Second Street across from present-day Cobb Drive in Colbert County, Alabama. The parents of Houston Cobb Sr. were Mack Griffin and Mattie Cobb, but they were never married. Mack eventually married Sally Cobb, the sister of Callie Cobb; therefore, Houston Cobb Sr. was given the maiden name of his mother, Mattie Cobb.

Mattie Cobb

Mattie was born in 1885 out of wedlock; her father was Shirley Eggleston and her mother was Callie Cobb who was born shortly after the Civil War in 1867. Since Shirley and Callie were never married, Mattie was given the last name of her mother, Callie Cobb.

Eggleston

Shirley Eggleston, the great-grandfather of Huston Cobb Jr., was probably a descendant of the Black slaves of Samuel O. Eggleston, a White plantation owner. Shirley Eggleston, a Black man, had a brother named Houston Eggleston. Houston may have been the namesake of Houston Cobb Sr. and Huston Cobb Jr.

In the 1850 Lawrence County, Alabama, Census, Samuel O. Eggleston was a 53-year-old White man from Virginia. Samuel was listed next to Amos Jarman in the census records.

In 1850, Samuel O. Eggleston was living in household 218, and he owned 48 Black slaves. The family of Samuel O. Eggleston included Eliza J. F. Eggleston, age 49, from Virginia; M. O. Eggleston, 21-year-old male, Alabama; M. L. Eggleston, 18-year-old male; Caroline U. Eggleston, age 16; Marcellus A. Eggleston, 13-year-old male; and William F. Eggleston, age nine.

Also in 1850, John L. Eggleston was 40 years old, and he was living in household 219 adjacent to Samuel O. Eggleston. He owned seven Black slaves. John L. Eggleston was the only White person in his household.

Archie Cobb

Callie Cobb was the great-grandmother Huston Cobb Jr.; she was the grandmother of Houston Cobb Sr. According to the 1870 census, Archie Cobb was 53 years old (Archie was 38 according to the 1880 census), and his daughter Callie was three years old, which indicates that she was born in 1867.

If the birth date of 1817 was correct, Archie Cobb was probably born a slave in Madison County of Alabama Territory. His Black family was probably descended from the slaves of a White cotton planter by the name of John B. Cobb. According to the land records, John B. Cobb first entered land in Madison County of Mississippi Territory around 1811.

On January 19, 1819, John B. Cobb entered land near Town Creek in Lawrence County, Alabama. Prior to 1895, the Town Creek Triangle was in Lawrence County. According to the 1830 Census of Lawrence County, Alabama, John B. Cobb owned 23 Black slaves.

The 1870 and 1880 federal census records indicate that Archie Cobb was born in Alabama which was made a territory on August 15, 1817; Alabama Territory was created out of Mississippi Territory. Whether he was born in 1817 or 1832, the parents of Archie Cobb were more than likely a Black slave family of the White plantation owner John B. Cobb.

Colbert County officially became a county in 1867. According to the 1870 Colbert County, Alabama, Census of the South Florence Post Office, Archie Cobb's family was listed as follows: 23/23, Cobb, Archie, age 53 (1880 census indicates he was born in 1832), male, Black, farm laborer, born in Alabama; Candas, age 30 (1880 census indicates she was born in 1833), female, Black, keeping house, born in Alabama; Bedford, age 16, male, Black, farm laborer, born in Alabama; Thomas, age 11, male, Black, born in Alabama; Malinda, age seven, female, Black, born in Alabama; Callie, age three, female, Black, born in Alabama; Salley; and, William, age 22, male, Black, farm laborer, born in Alabama.

Archie Cobb died in 1905 near Leighton in Colbert County, Alabama. Archie probably lived his boyhood life as a slave on cotton plantations in present-day Colbert County, Alabama. The Leighton newspaper reported his death. According to *The Leighton News*, April 28, 1905, Volume 14, No. 10, "Old Uncle Archie Cobb...died last Sunday evening. Peace to his ashes."

Mack Griffin

The mother of Mack Griffin was Mary Griffin from Moulton in Lawrence County, Alabama. The Black Griffin Family probably got their family name from a White cotton planter by the name of G. W. Griffin. According to the 1850 slave census of Lawrence County, Alabama, G. W. Griffin owned nine Black slaves.

Mack Griffin was probably born in Moulton, and he died in 1923. Mack was originally buried at Mount Pleasant Cemetery on the County Line Road just south of present-day Ford City. After the burial of his body for 83 years, his remains were exhumed and moved. In 2006, Mack Griffin was reinterred in the Cobb Family Cemetery behind Bethel Church on Highway 184 or Second Street.

After Mack Griffin, father of Houston Cobb Sr., and his wife Salley Cobb Griffin died, Houston Cobb Sr. inherited half of the 42 acres of land that his biological father and great-aunt Salley owned. Salley was the sister of Houston Cobb Sr.'s grandmother, Callie Cobb. Houston Cobb Sr. inherited 21 acres of land that was just south of Second Street near the longtime home of Huston Cobb Jr.

Family of Houston Sr.

Houston Cobb Sr. and Nazareth Carter Cobb had the following children:
1. Tracien Cobb was born on October 15, 1923. She married John W. Oates (1901–1965) on June 8, 1948. Tracien Cobb Oates died on January 15, 2020; she was buried in Zion Number 1 Missionary Baptist Church Cemetery at Barton in Colbert County, Alabama.

2. Huston Cobb Jr. was born on March 10, 1925; he married Sadie Long.

3. Leo Mack Cobb was born on October 27, 1927; in 1951, he married Nazerine Jarman. Leo died on October 14, 2018, and he was buried in the Houston Cobb Sr. Family Cemetery at Bethel in Colbert County, Alabama.

4. Earnest Cobb was born on July 7,1929; he married Helen Mary Stanley. Earnest died on September 27, 2000, and he was buried in the Houston Cobb Sr. Family Cemetery at Bethel in Colbert County, Alabama.

5. Carl Elbert Cobb was born on April 13, 1931; in 1955, he married Anita Smith. Carl died on December 17, 2014, and he was buried in the Houston Cobb Sr. Family Cemetery at Bethel in Colbert County, Alabama.

6. Mattie Cleazell Cobb was born on January 29, 1933; she married Harry Long Jr. Mattie Cleazell Cobb died on May 18, 2022.

7. Willie I. Cobb was born on December 13, 1934. He lives in Romulus, Michigan.

Hog Island

Tracien Cobb, the sister of Huston Cobb Jr., was born on October 16, 1923, on Hog Island in the mouth of Town Creek prior to the flooding of the area by Wilson Dam and Lake. Wilson Lake was the first impoundment on the Tennessee River. Construction of Wilson Dam began in 1918 and the dam was completed in 1924. The dam was named for former President of the United States Woodrow Wilson.

Front: Earnest, Leo Mack, Carl, Huston, and Willie
Back: Tracien and Mattie
January 23, 1998

Houston and Nazareth Carter Cobb, along with other Black families, lived and farmed on Hog Island before the rising flood waters inundated the island when Wilson Dam was closed. Houston was a young man of 22 years old when he and his family were forced to move from their home on Hog Island. Just prior to the flooding of the reservoir, the Houston Cobb Family moved just a mile south near Second Street where Huston Cobb Jr. was born.

Hog Island probably got its name from the Hogg Family found in the area during the 1870 census. Traditionally, many of the islands in the Tennessee River were named for the White settler families that owned or lived on the islands after the Indians were removed.

Prior to Indian removal from the area in 1816, the

area around Hog Island was in the Cherokee village called Shoal Town. Originally, the site was a large prehistoric Indian settlement with several large mounds on Hog Island dating back to the Archaic Period. The historic Shoal Town included the area of Hog Island in the mouth of (Shoal) Town Creek, and also the mouths of Blue Water Creek and Big Nance's Creek on the Big Muscle Shoals of the Tennessee River.

Chickamauga Cherokee Chief Doublehead moved from Doublehead's Town at the Browns Ferry crossing of the Tennessee River in present-day Lawrence County, Alabama, to Shoal Town in 1802. Lower Cherokee Chiefs Doublehead and Kattygisky lived at Shoal Town which included Hog Island. Doublehead was assassinated on August 9, 1807.

Shoal Town was the largest Chickamauga Cherokee town in the area and was the home of Doublehead, Kattygisky, Tahluntuskee (Talohuskee) Benge, and John D. Chisholm. In January 1810 because of fear of assassination like his Uncle Doublehead, Tahluntuskee led his Lower Cherokee people from their home at Shoal Town to west of the Mississippi River and became known as the "Cherokees West" or "Old Settlers."

The Hog Island area where Tracien was born and where Houston and Nazareth Carter Cobb once lived was abandoned by the Indians after the 1816 Turkey Town Treaty took the land from the Cherokees. In 1818, cotton planters from Virginia and North Carolina brought their families and Black slaves to the area in search of the rich alluvial soils along the Tennessee River.

Today, the first home place on Hog Island of Houston and his wife Nazareth is presently covered with some two to four feet of shallow backwaters of Wilson Lake. The island is located about two miles west of present-day Wheeler Dam near the middle of Big Muscle Shoals. Hog Island is located adjacent to the south edge of the main channel of the Tennessee River in the mouth of Town Creek; the island was about a mile north of Kittiakaska Creek.

Kittiakaska Creek

During the time that Huston Cobb Jr. was a young boy, Kittiakaska Creek was used as a water supply for the Houston Cobb Sr. Family. The big spring that supplied water to the creek was about one-half mile southwest of Hog Island.

Huston said, "We loaded the water from the creek just a few hundred yards east of the big spring flowing into Kittiakaska Creek. The spring never went dry and was always a good source of water. We would put barrels in our mule-pulled wagon and go to the creek during dry weather to get water for our livestock."

Kittiakaska Creek that crossed by the cotton plantation home of John H. Johnson was named in honor of the Lower Cherokee Chief Kattygisky. Huston Cobb Jr. said, "The last name of my great-grandfather, Martin Johnson Jr., came from my ancestors who were slaves of John H. Johnson."

The area just west of Kattygisky's Spring become the home of John H. Johnson of Virginia. John was the father-in-law of Lewis Dillahunty, who was sent to the area in 1816 to secure the peaceful removal of the Cherokees.

Huston Cobb Jr. and I at the John Johnson home

The small creek runs into Town Creek about a half mile south of the Tennessee River in Section 26 of Township 3 South, and Range 9 West. The creek had several different spellings of the name on various maps including Kittikaski, Kittikaskia, Kitticaski, Kitticaska, Killycasidda, Kittycasidda, and Kitticaski; it was no different with the Cherokee Chief Kattygisky whose name was spelled a dozen different ways.

Today, the mouth of Kittiakaska Creek is west of present-day Doublehead Resort. The present-day River Road in Colbert County crosses the creek in sight of the resort. The Indian trail was known as the South River Road, which ran along the south bank of the Tennessee River through the State of Alabama. About three-fourths of a mile west of the mouth of Kittiakaska Creek is the large Kattygisky Spring, which was earlier the home of the Cherokee Chief Kattygisky.

Willie A. Ashford

Huston said, "The creek was also used as a baptizing

hole for the Bethel Colbert Baptist Church. Lorene Rutland and I were baptized in the creek in 1935 by Reverend Willie A. Ashford." The baptizing hole was located in the center of Section 26 of Township 3 South and Range 9 West.

According to Huston Cobb, "The baptizing hole on Kittiakaska Creek was about three to four feet deep. The blue hole was up the creek about a half of mile from the baptizing hole. Later, the church started baptizing people at the old Foster's Bridge on Town Creek."

Huston continued, "Reverend Willie A. Ashford was the preacher at the Bethel Colbert Baptist Church, and he would ride a train from Courtland to Town Creek. When I turned 16 years old, I would pick up Ashford at the railroad station in the Town of Town Creek and bring him to our home on Saturday."

Willie A. Ashford was probably a descendant of the Black slaves of Major Thomas Harrison Ashford Sr. of Virginia. His cotton plantation, known as Free and Easy, was near Courtland and consisted of some 1,400 acres of land. According to the 1850 slave census of Lawrence County, Alabama, Major Ashford owned 48 Black slaves.

Huston continued, "Reverend Ashford would preach on Sunday at Bethel Colbert Church, which was on the south fork of Kittiakaska Creek and Second Street. After the noon service, I would carry him back to the railroad station at Town Creek to catch a train back to Courtland.

"In addition to Reverend Ashford, teachers that taught at the one-room Bethel School would also board with our family (Houston Cobb Sr.) during the week, and they would go home on the weekend. Bethel School was located across the road from Bethel Church and just south of Second Street. Most of the teachers would come from Sheffield or Tuscumbia to teach at the one-room school that was for the nearby Black children."

1940 Census

According to the 1940 Colbert County, Alabama, Census, Houston Cobb Sr., head of Household 216, was a 36-year-old Black male farmer. The following were listed in his household: Nazareth, wife, 36; Tracien, daughter, 16; Huston, son, 14; Leo Mack, son, 12; Earnest, son, 10; Carl, son, nine; Mattie C., daughter, six; and Willie Irvin, son, five.

Also living in the household in 1940 with Houston Cobb were his cousins as follows: Marcella Newsome, cousin, male, 25; Geneva, cousin, female, 21; Gladys M., cousin, female, four; Rosella, cousin, female, three. At the time, Houston was living next to Ocie and Elsie Lee King Stanley in household number 217.

In 1940, Huston Cobb Jr. was only 14 years old, but he was expected to contribute to the family chores. Huston did all kinds of daily tasks without being told; he knew his duties were important in maintaining the home of his father, mother, siblings, and cousins.

Foster's Mill

Some of the slave ancestors of Mr. Huston Cobb Jr. lived in the Town Creek Triangle and spent much of their lives in the area of Foster's Mill. According to a 1908 map of Colbert County, Foster's Mill was located near the junction of Kittiakaska Creek and Town Creek. It was at this location that records show that Mary C. Foster owned the land on both sides of the River Road. The grist mill was owned by Thomas Jefferson Foster, but the relationship to Mary C. Foster was unknown.

According to the 1860 slave census of Lawrence County, Alabama, Thomas Jefferson Foster owned 129 Black slaves. Many of the Black folks living in or near the Town Creek Triangle, Foster's Mill, Red Bank, and other places along the river are descendants of the slaves of the White Foster cotton planters who owned land in the area: Thomas J. Foster, George Foster, Davie Foster, John Foster, M. L. Foster, and Washington Foster.

Foster's Mill was the original name of the bridge crossing Town Creek at Doublehead Resort; however, today the bridge is now called Joe Patterson Bridge. The road that crosses Town Creek and runs past Doublehead Resort is still called Foster's Mill Road. Foster's Mill Road was initially known as the River Road, an ancient Indian path; today, the route is still known as the River Road.

White King Family

The King Family was one of the roughly 30 original groups of White slave-owning cotton planters that came to the Colbert County area of Alabama from North Carolina and Virginia. According to the 1860 slave census, the King Family in the area owned some 325 Black slaves.

During the days of slavery, the King Family accumulated fine homes, farms, businesses, many acres of land, and considerable wealth for that time. Many of the Black folks in the Colbert County portion of northwest Alabama are descendants of the slaves of the King Family. Some of the Black descendants of the slaves remained in Colbert County area after the Civil War.

Huston said, "Claude King, a White man, owned a cotton gin and two stores in Leighton, and one store in Florence. Claude furnished both Black and White farmers in the area. Some members of the King Family maintained their wealth after the Civil War and continued to have economic ties to their former Black slaves. The King Family provided the materials and backing to the small Black farmers in exchange for mortgages on everything they owned."

Huston continued, "Many of the poor White and Black families had to mortgage their property in order to make a crop. Therefore, during bad harvest years, these marginal families lost their property to the wealthy White folks that held their mortgage.

"Especially during the years of the Great Depression, the wealthy got richer while many of the small landowners lost everything they had accumulated. The vicious cycle of poverty, low wages, poor living conditions, and other factors of economic depression continued during the depression until the New Deal under Roosevelt and other social programs put the poor Whites and Blacks on better footing for improved living conditions."

Houston's Car

According to Huston Cobb Jr., "In 1929, my daddy, Houston Cobb Sr., and Salley Cobb Griffin (Houston's stepmother and great-aunt) bought a 1929 Chevrolet car when Republican Herbert Hoover took office as President of the United States. During the Hoover presidency, the United States economy plunged into the Great Depression. The financial situation of the country continued to get worse until Democrat Franklin D. Roosevelt won the presidential election in 1932 at the depth of the depression."

**Nazareth Carter Cobb, Huston Cobb Sr., Sally Cobb Griffin
1929 Cheverolet–1/4 mile southwest of Bethel Colbert Church**

Huston continued, "The 1929 car was purchased from Emmitt King of Leighton; Emmitt was the son of Claude King. The car daddy owned was the only new car owned by a Black family. Both Black and White folks would come to the home of my daddy seeking transportation within the area. They would get him to carry them to doctors, funerals, or even dates for young men to see their girlfriends."

Tennessee Valley Authority

Huston Cobb Jr. continued, "Immediately after being elected President of the United States, Roosevelt began the New Deal, which came up with programs that included the Tennessee Valley Authority (TVA). Among the work projects of TVA was the construction of Wheeler Dam, which was started in January 1933 and completed November 9, 1936."

"My daddy, Houston Cobb Sr., got a job at Wheeler Dam in 1934. He made thirty-five cents per hour working on the dam and received a check every two weeks. He worked on the dam until it was completed. While working for TVA at Wheeler Dam, he ran a jack hammer."

Huston stated, "After completing work on Wheeler Dam, my daddy Houston began work at the nitric plant number two near Wilson Dam in present-day Muscle Shoals, Alabama. Wilson Dam was started in 1918 and completed in 1924 by the Army Corps of Engineers, but the dam became part of the TVA in 1933. Wilson Dam was originally built to provide power to the nitrate plants that were built to make explosives for World War I."

Huston Cobb Jr. said, "My daddy made a good living working with TVA, but he also farmed. Most farming seasons, he would borrow $300.00 a year to make a crop. In order to get the money for the crop, he had to mortgage our property. We really did not know we were poor, but we were better off than most Black and White families. My family went to church every Sunday, and many of the TVA workers would wear their badge to church to show that they had a job."

Death of Houston Cobb Sr.

On October 24, 1985, Houston died on the south side of Second Street in the Town Creek Triangle in Colbert County, Alabama.  He was buried in the Houston Cobb Sr. Family Cemetery near Bethel Colbert Church Community in Colbert County. Houston had lived his entire life within a few miles from where he was born.

Nazareth Carter Cobb

Huston Cobb Jr. said, "My mother was Nazareth Carter Cobb. The father of Nazareth was Tracy C. Carter, who was born in October 1878, and her mother was Fannie Johnson who was born in August 1883."

Huston added, "My mother, Nazareth Carter, was born on November 3, 1902. She had the following brothers and sisters: Carl A. (Boss) Carter, Willie Dee Carter, Caroline Carter, Mary Alice Carter, Mattie Ellen Carter, Annie Lee Carter, Jimmy B. Carter, and Odessa Carter."

Huston Cobb Jr. and Nazareth

Huston continued, "Nazareth attended Courtland Academy, which was a Black boarding school at Courtland in Lawrence County, Alabama. She attended the academy until the eighth grade; the school burned in 1928. The academy was built by a group of Black churches organized as the North Alabama Baptist Association."

Huston said, "Tracy and Fannie Johnson Carter initially lived in the Town Creek Triangle on the John H. Johnson farm. The land was previously known as The

71

Green Onion Plantation. Their home was about one-half mile southwest of the mouth of Town Creek."

Green Onion Plantation

The grandmother of Huston Cobb Jr. was Fannie Johnson, the daughter of Martin Johnson Jr. The Martin Johnson Jr. farm was also located on part of the old Green Onion Plantation near the mouth of Town Creek in present-day Colbert County, Alabama.

The Black family of Martin Johnson were the descendants of the Black slaves of the plantation of John H. Johnson. The Johnson plantation home was about a half mile southwest of the mouth of the Kittiakaska Creek and about 200 yards west of Kittiakaska Spring.

John Johnson Plantation House

Huston Cobb Jr. said, "According to local folklore, a rope and pulley system was used to pull water from the spring to the John H. Johnson house on the hilltop. Johnson had built the large tidewater brick home just west of the present-day junction of the Foster's Mill Road and the River Road."

On a visit to the John H. Johnson home, Mr. Cobb and I saw that the walls were some three or more layers of brick thick. The house was in the process of decay and disrepair, with the west wall fallen, and the back of the house seen in the picture below is gone.

The site was listed in 1850 as "The Green Onion Plantation"; today, it is still known by that name. Mr. Cobb said, "Later, during prohibition, The Green Onion was the site of an alcoholic establishment of a local bootlegger near the mouth of Kittiakaska Creek."

John H. Johnson

Captain John H. Johnson of Virginia was married three times; his wives were Elizabeth Williams, Nancy, and an unknown wife. Supposedly, on August 3, 1807, Captain John H. Johnson and Nancy leased 1,000 acres from Doublehead in an agreement between John D. Chisholm and the State of Georgia. However, on August 9, 1807, Doublehead was assassinated and his leases to White settlers came into question especially with the Chickasaw Indians. The Chickasaw petitioned the United States Government to remove all White settlers from Chickasaw land. In order to comply with the Chickasaw request, the government built Fort Hampton in Limestone County, which was established to remove White squatters.

Before 1830, John H. Johnson's daughter, Maredian, who was born in Virginia in 1806, married Cordial Faircloth.

In the 1820 Census of Lawrence County, Cordial Faircloth's household located in the Town Creek Triangle was listed as having one male over 21, one female over 21, two males under 21, and three Black slaves. According to the 1850 slave census, Cordial Faircloth had 38 Black slaves. The Faircloth Family lived between the River Road and the Tennessee River north of the John H. Johnson place.

Another daughter of John H. Johnson, Lucinda, married Major Lewis Dillahunty; in 1816, Major Dillahunty and Lucinda came into North Alabama. Dillahunty, on the request of General Andrew Jackson, was sent to this area by the fifth President of the United States James Monroe in 1816 to secure removal of the Indians on the south side of the Tennessee River. He was to survey the Indian lands and secure these lands for the United States.

Lewis and Lucinda Dillahunty were the first residents of Courtland, Alabama. In the 1820 census, the Lewis Dillahunty household had the following: a male and female over 21; two females under 21; and three Black slaves. In 1820, Thomas Dillahunty was listed as having nine black slaves.

Major Dillahunty assisted with the removal of the Indians from northwest Alabama including the Town Creek Triangle area. On September 16 and 18, 1816, both the Cherokees and Chickasaws signed the Turkey Town Treaty giving up their overlapping claims to the land on the south side of the Tennessee River. The Chickasaws received $120,000 and the Cherokees were paid $60,000 for the land in which includes the present-day counties of Colbert, Franklin, Lawrence, and Morgan.

Since John Johnson was in Alabama just prior to

Doublehead's death, his family was probably familiar with the Town Creek area. These Indian lands were sold during the federal lands sales starting in September of 1818. According to local folklore, Major Dillahunty selected the area at Kittiakaska Spring for the home of his father-in-law, John H. Johnson.

The Green Onion Plantation of John H. Johnson included the land south of the mouth of Town Creek between the north and south forks of Kittikaski Branch. The Johnson

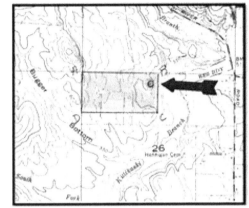

The Green Onion

place was north of Second Street and west of the River Road. Originally, all the John H. Johnson land was part of Lawrence County, Alabama. In 1895, the area of Lawrence County west of Town Creek, north of the Franklin County line, and east of the County Line Road that ran through White Oak, Leighton, and Ford City was annexed into Colbert County.

John H. Johnson had a son John T. Johnson; another man, John A. Johnson of Colbert County, may be a descendant of the Johnson Family of The Green Onion. The 1870 census of Colbert County shows the following: John A. Johnson, age 41, male, White, farm laborer, born in AL; Mary, age 30, female, White, keeping house, born in AL; Isaac, age 12, male, White, farm laborer, born in AL; Thomas, age 10, male, White, at home, born in AL; Newton, age nine, male, White, at home, born in AL; Joshua, age eight, male, White, at home, born in AL; Martha, age four, female, White, born in AL; Lawranci, age 63, female, White, at home, born in GA.

In the 1880 Colbert County, Alabama, Census, John A. Johnson was living in Tuscumbia with the following: Mary was listed as Mary E.; Isaac L.; Robert N.; Joshua W.; and Martha A. Johnson.

According to the 1850 slave census, the Johnsons of northeast Colbert County had some 20 Black slaves that were the ancestors of many Black folks in area including the family of Huston Cobb Jr. Also in 1850, the agent for The Green Onion, or the John H. Johnson plantation, was listed as being Thomas Jefferson Foster; at that time, he had under his control some 95 Black slaves.

Martin Johnson

According to family folklore, Martin Johnson Sr. was a Black slave of John H. Johnson. Martin was born a slave in 1820, and he was the great-great-grandfather of Huston Cobb Jr.

Martin Johnson Jr. was the son of Martin Johnson Sr. They settled in the Town Creek Triangle area around the mouth of Town Creek prior to 1820. Many of the Black slaves of John H. Johnson took his last name.

Martin Johnson Jr. was born a slave of the White family of John H. Johnson about 1849. Martin Johnson Jr. was the maternal great-grandfather of Huston Cobb Jr. Martin was 21 years old in the 1870 Census of Colbert County, Alabama.

The maternal grandfather of Nazareth Carter was Martin Johnson Jr.; Nazareth was the daughter of Fannie Johnson. Nazareth was born on the home place of Martin Johnson Jr., which was located in the northeast corner of the junction of Second Street and Mt. Stanley Road.

Today, the Mt. Stanley Road actually has its beginning on Second Street and ends at the River Road to the north. The old home site of Martin Johnson Jr. was on a beautiful hilltop near the road crossing that was visible south of the mouth of Town Creek and the Tennessee River in present-day Colbert County, Alabama.

The grandmother of Huston Cobb Jr. was Fannie Johnson, the daughter of Martin Johnson Jr. Martin Jr. married Caroline, who was a Mulatto that was half-Black and half-White. Caroline was the great-grandmother of Huston Cobb Jr.

Huston Cobb Jr. said, "The mother of Caroline was a Black slave and her father was White; the White father was either an overseer or the slave owner. The mother of Caroline was a Black slave, and her name was Viney. In her later years, Viney lived with Martin and Caroline."

Martin Johnson Jr. owned 52 acres of land; Martin bought the land and lived just northeast of the River Road and Second Street. He lived in the Town Creek Triangle from about 1849 until his death in 1928. Caroline, the wife of Martin Johnson Jr., named Huston Cobb Jr. Martin and his wife Caroline were buried in the Bethel Colbert Missionary Baptist Church Cemetery in the Town Creek Triangle.

Tracy C. Carter

Tracy C. Carter was the father of Nazareth Carter Cobb. Tracy was the son of Cyrus (Sye) Carter and Mary Alice Carter; he married Fannie Johnson. Tracy and Fannie Johnson Carter were the maternal grandparents of Huston Cobb Jr. Their last name Carter came from the White cotton planter family of Ammon Carter. The Carters owned the Black slaves from whom Cyrus Carter descended.

Huston Cobb Jr. said, "My grandfather, Tracy C. Carter, was a farmer. Tracy fired the boiler for the cotton gin on the River Road about a quarter mile north of Second Street. He worked for Will Norman at the cotton gin, and he fired the gin boiler with wood to make steam to run the mill."

Huston added, "Tracy Carter got his arm caught in the belt running the cotton gin and broke his arm in several places. It took a long time for him to heal, but he finally got well from the accident without losing his arm."

Huston continued, "When Caroline Johnson died, Martin Johnson Jr. moved in with his daughter, Fannie Johnson Carter, and his son-in-law, Tracy Carter. Martin lived with his daughter Fannie and Tracy Carter until his death. After Martin died, his 52 acres of land were divided up among his descendants. Tracy Carter was administrator of farm of Martin Johnson Jr. The descendants of Martin sold the land and divided the money equally.

"Tracy and Fannie Carter lost their place when the gin owner Will Norman died. At the time of Norman's death, Tracy Carter was making payments on the five acres of land; however, since Tracy did not have a legal deed, the children of Will Norman reclaimed the property.

"Tracy and Fannie Carter lost the five acres that they were in the process of buying in the Town Creek Triangle at northwest corner of the junction of the Mt. Stanley Road and Second Street. After their loss, the Tracy Carter Family moved about one mile west on Second Street."

Huston Cobb Jr. continued, "My maternal grandparents, Tracy and Fannie Johnson Carter, used Buck Bridge going to the town of Town Creek to trade with a man by the name of Streeter. He was furnishing farming supplies to my grandfather, Tracy Carter. During the Great Depression of the early 1930s, my Carter grandparents lost everything they had. They lost their property to Streeter including a 1928 Ford, mules, and wagon."

Cyrus (Sye) Carter

Cyrus (Sye) Carter and Mary Alice Carter were the maternal great-grandparents of Huston Cobb Jr. Sye and Mary Carter lived in the Town Creek Triangle of Colbert County, Alabama, and they worked on the Carter Plantation.

The father of Cyrus Carter lived near the Tennessee River, and he was a slave of the Carter Family. One day, Cyrus' daddy just disappeared, and no one ever knew what happened to him. Huston Cobb Jr. said, "My great-great-grandfather could have been killed, thrown in the Tennessee River, or could have possibly escaped north, but my family always believed the worse. We feel he was killed by his slaveholder overseer or owner."

Cyrus Carter was last listed on the 1880 census; by the 1900 census, only Mary Alice, wife of Cyrus, was listed as the head of the household. Therefore, Cyrus must have died between 1880 and 1900. Cyrus and Mary Alice had 16 children.

Cyrus (Sye) and Mary Alice Carter are buried a few miles south of Ford City at Mount Pleasant Cemetery on the County Line Road. Huston Cobb Jr. showed me the tombstone of his great-grandfather Cyrus (Sye) Carter at the huge Mount Pleasant Cemetery on the east side of County Line Road.

Carter Plantation

The oldest of the White cotton planter family of Carters to migrate to the Town Creek Triangle was Ammon Carter. Ammon was born in Buckingham County, Virginia, in 1765, and he died on October 20, 1851, in what was then Lawrence County, Alabama. He and his family brought their Black slaves from Virginia to the Triangle.

In the 1850 Census of Lawrence County, Ammon Carter was listed as being 85 years old from Virginia. Ammon was buried just to the north of the Jarman Plantation Home and just a few yards south of the River Road in the Hatton Baptist Cemetery in present-day Colbert County, Alabama.

Ammon was married to Mary "Polly" Burnett who was also born in Virginia, on August 8, 1773, and died in Lawrence County, Alabama, on October 19, 1837. Ammon and Mary had the following six children: Joel Walker Jones Carter, Ammon Carter Jr., David B. Carter, Sabra or Mary Carter, Mahala Carter, and Samuel Carter.

In the 1860 slave census of Lawrence County, the Carters owned 50 Black slaves. Joel Walker Jones Carter, son of Ammon Carter, was listed in the 1860 Census of Lawrence County, Alabama, as being a 65-year-old farmer from Virginia; at the time, he owned 31 Black slaves. His family included Sarah, age 65, from Tennessee; John D., 42-year-old farmer from Tennessee; Nancy, age 42, Tennessee; J. N. McCarley, age 29, merchant from Tennessee; Eliza E., age 30, Tennessee; Lern Carter, 27 year old male farmer from Alabama; Anna, age 20, Alabama; P. P., 18 year old male student from Alabama; Alice, age 13, Alabama; J. W., ten-year-old female, Alabama; Mary, age eight, Alabama; Jere, six-year-old male, Alabama; and Marcellus, two-year-old male, Alabama.

Black Carter Family

The Black Carter Family were the descendants of the Black slaves of the White Carter Family from Virginia. The Carter Place was in the Town Creek Triangle between the River Road and Tennessee River. Their cotton plantation was north to northeast of the Amos Jarman Plantation and present-day Ford City.

After the Civil War, many of the former Black slave families stayed in the Town Creek Triangle on or near the plantation or farm where they were born. This is why some of the family of Huston Cobb Jr. is still in the same area of Colbert County, Alabama.

Some of the Black slaves that were the ancestors of Huston Cobb Jr. remained near where they lived and worked on the cotton plantations of their former owners after the Civil War. Many times, these former slaves continued to work for their plantation owners after the war.

Death of Nazareth Carter Cobb

Nazareth Carter Cobb, the mother of Huston Cobb Jr., spent the majority of her life in the Town Creek Triangle of present-day Colbert County, Alabama. Nazareth died on April 24, 1962; she passed away some 23 years before her husband Houston Cobb Sr. passed in 1985. She was buried in the Houston Cobb Sr. Cemetery near where she lived her life.

Huston Cobb Jr.

On March 10, 1925, Huston Cobb Jr. was born to Houston Cobb Sr. and Nazareth Carter Cobb. Huston Cobb was delivered by Dr. W. H. Stanley for $14.00. Stanley was a White country doctor that attended patients in a horse drawn buggy. Huston was born at home only one and a half miles from where he lived most of his life.

Huston Cobb Jr., Leo Cobb, Ernest Cobb, Tracien Cobb 1930–1/4 mile southwest of Bethel Colbert Baptist Church

Doctor Stanley, who delivered Huston Cobb Jr., lived on Mt. Stanley Road, which ran from Second Street and Sixth Street in Colbert County. According to the 1860 Lawrence County census records, the White Stanley Family members owned 53 Black slaves.

Huston Cobb Jr. said, "During my school days, I had to help on the family farm. After school each day, I would put on my work clothes and do my chores until dark. My family had a dug well where we got our drinking water and wash water for the big cast iron pot. I had to draw water from the well to use for the household.

"My family planted cotton as the main cash crop. I plowed the cotton fields with mules and a turning plow, scratcher, and Georgia stock. I also had to hoe weeds out of my family's cotton fields. As a young man, I could pick 300 pounds of cotton per day. We would make 12 to 15 bales of cotton per year, which sold for twenty-five to thirty cents per pound.

"My folks planted two to three acres of peas which had to be picked and shelled. We also planted peanuts, some of which were carried to the market to sell. Each year, our family made 150 gallons of molasses from two to three acres of sugarcane that we planted. Each spring, my family planted a big garden and raised most of the food we ate."

Huston continued, "I had to help cut hay to feed the mules and cows. I also took care of the other farm animals. My family had two pairs of mules, and they had to be fed each night; the mules were named Blue, Annie, and Nell. The mules were an important part of the farm work.

"I milked two cows and gathered eggs from all kinds of chickens that my family owned. My folks also had a couple of sows to raise a bunch of pigs. Each year, four to five head of hogs were fattened to be killed, which provided meat throughout the winter. I turned the sausage grinder to process some of the pork for breakfast meat.

"We had a big orchard with peaches, apples, cherries, pears, and big grape harbor. All kinds of fruit were dried on top of the house porch roof during the summer and fall. Our family had some pecan trees that provided nuts to eat each fall. We also had a hand-cranked ice cream freezer which made some of the best eating during the hot summer and fall months."

Huston Cobb Jr. continued, "In late 1930, my family had a two-row drill planter, a mowing machine for hay cutting, and a new mule-drawn Webber wagon. My step-granddad was William Henry Fuqua; he was a blacksmith and repaired the farming equipment. My daddy plowed with a pair of mules most of his life.

"The closest grocery store was about two miles east of our home in northwest corner of Mt. Stanley Road and Second Street. Not far west of where we lived was Austin's Mill, which was run by kerosene. My daddy would take corn to grind into meal, which was paid for by giving a portion of the meal for the grinding. Austin's Mill was west of Brick Hatton School about one-quarter of a mile."

According to Huston Cobb Jr., "The Cobb Family consisted of the two parents and four children; the first house we lived in was only two rooms and was on a log foundation. To get from one room to the other room, we had to go out on porch; the rooms were not connected by a door. In order to keep our family warm in the wintertime, I had cut wood for the fireplace with an ax and crosscut saw. From our little two-room home, my family moved into Salley Cobb Griffin's house after she died; we used kerosene lamps for light at night and early morning."

Huston continued, "When I was a young boy, Foster's Bridge and Buck Bridge were the only two crossings of Town Creek in the Town Creek Triangle area. Buck Bridge was named because of a buck deer being killed at the bridge while the bridge was being built; the buck was swimming down the creek. The original Buck Bridge fell in with a load of cotton and was rebuilt."

Huston and Sadie Cobb

Across the road and just west of Bethel Colbert Baptist Church was a one-room school that Huston Cobb Jr. attended. The Black school was on the south side of Second Street only a quarter mile east of where Huston lived most of his life.

In 1938 at the age of 12, Huston Cobb Jr. transferred from the one-room school near Bethel Colbert Baptist Church. He started at the Leighton Training School in Leighton, Alabama, which was for only Black students.

At Leighton Training School, Carrie Pierce was the first teacher of Huston Cobb Jr. Ms. Pierce told the students to write Ms. Sadie Long a letter telling her they missed her at school.

The parents of Sadie Long were Harry Long and Mary Long. The siblings of Sadie were Mable Long, Mildred Long, Pearl Long, Dorothy Long, Bobbie Jean Long, Harry Long Jr., and John Lewis (Buddy) Long. After their deaths, Harry and Mary Long were interned in the Pearsall Cemetery, which was near their home. The cemetery was located on Ford Road which connects Second Street and the River Road; Ford Road is just southeast of Stinson Hollow on Wilson Lake in Colbert County, Alabama.

Initially, Sadie Long had attended Ricks School at The Oaks which was held in the Mother Church. It was not known where Sadie Long was born, but it is sure that she attended the Black school at Mother Church within a few hundred yards south of plantation house known as The Oaks.

Sadie Long

Sadie Long went to school in the second building that was on the site of the Mother Church; the first building had to be rebuilt. The school and church were actually held in the same building on The Oaks Plantation of Abraham Ricks. The Black school, also known as Ricks School, at The Oaks finally closed in 1937.

After her school at The Oaks Plantation was closed, Sadie started at Leighton Training School. The school for Black students was located on the west side of Leighton in Colbert County, Alabama.

When his teacher asked everyone to write Sadie, Huston Cobb Jr. eagerly penned a letter to Sadie Long as other students also did. However, Sadie related that the letter Huston sent did not mean much at the time because she did not know him and had never made his acquaintance.

At the time of the class letter-writing assignment, Sadie was 12 years old and Huston was 13 years old. When

Huston wrote his letter to Sadie Long, he did not know Sadie, and he had never met her.

At the time Sadie Long started attending school at Leighton, she was living with her family in Wooten Field, which was located approximately one and one-half miles south of Second Street and about three miles southeast of present-day Constellium (previously Wise and Reynolds).

Shortly after receiving the letters, Sadie started back at Leighton Training School. At the time, the school was one of the finest in the county for Black students.

Leighton Training School Before

After Sadie started coming to Leighton in the sixth grade in 1938, Huston and Sadie walked together when their class attended a picnic. Sadie claimed that she walked fast trying to out distance Huston, but he managed to keep pace. Shortly after the class picnic in the spring of the year, Huston sent Sadie a personal postcard which her sister intercepted and read before Sadie. After she received the sweet card from Huston, Sadie allowed him to claim her as his girlfriend.

The best friend of Huston Cobb was Frank Hall,

who had claimed a girl that was the good friend of Sadie. After some three years of claiming each other, Frank asked Sadie if she and Huston Cobb Jr. were still going to claim each other. Sadie replied that she was not studying Huston.

When word got to Huston, he said that he was not studying Sadie either, and the couple of three years begin drifting apart. The initial romance really began to fall apart when Sadie transferred to Sheffield, and Huston stayed at Leighton.

Military Service

During his senior year, Huston Cobb was drafted in 1944, and he joined the United States Navy. Huston said, "It was about the time for me to graduate from high school when I was drafted. While the rest of my class was walking across the stage to receive their high school diplomas, I was in the Navy serving at Pearl Harbor, Hawaii; however, I was allowed to graduate. My daddy, Houston Cobb Sr. received my diploma in my absence."

While stationed in Hawaii, Huston was a naval stevedore. His main job was loading and unloading ships at Pearl Harbor from 1944 until April 1946.

During his tour of duty in the Navy, Huston wrote his friend Frank Hall, who happened to share the

Huston Cobb Jr.
U.S. Navy 1945

letter he received with Sadie Long. Frank encouraged Sadie to write to Huston which she did; Huston quickly replied to the letter from Sadie.

The couple revived a long-forgotten romance through their letter correspondence. In one letter received from Huston, Sadie was concerned about a phrase that stated they should become one. This letter can be seen in Appendix B. Huston and Sadie kept all the letters written while he was serving in the Navy.

In 1945 while Huston was serving in the Navy, United States President Harry S. Truman by executive order

 desegregated Blacks and Whites in the military. Even though President Truman tried to desegregate the Blacks and Whites serving in the United States military, it appeared to Huston that many of the White soldiers did all that they could to keep Blacks and Whites segregated.

Huston spent two years in Hawaii and got back home exactly two years from the day he left. When he was discharged in April 1946 from the United States Navy, Huston got three hundred dollars in compensation from the military for his service.

When his service in Hawaii was completed, Huston

rode back from Pearl Harbor with the White soldiers; however, all servicemen had to sleep on stretchers in the bottom of the ship. It took five to six days on the ship to get from Pearl Harbor to the mainland in California.

When Huston Cobb Jr. got back to California, he went to Memphis, Tennessee. He had to be aware of the color requirements for drinking and using the bathroom. Blacks had to use certain facilities separate from the Whites. In civilian life, it was still the segregation of the old days, and it did not change until the 1960s.

Therefore, when Huston Cobb Jr. got back home after two years of honorable service in the United States Navy, he had to observe the rules of segregation. He had ride in the back of the bus, could not drink from the same water fountain as Whites, could not eat with White folks, or go in some White establishments.

After getting out of the Navy, Huston Cobb Jr. gave George Eggleston $130.00 for a horse which George had mortgaged. Huston stalled his vehicle and George charged him $5.00 to pull him out of the mud. Later, George's brother told him that he could not sell a mortgaged horse. George told Huston that he wanted to buy the horse he had mortgaged. Houston sold him the horse for $135.00; therefore, they broke even.

Later, Huston bought a tractor which he and his brothers used for at least two years. Huston sold the first tractor and bought a Farmall H; he farmed with the Farmall for several years.

Huston's Family

After getting home in 1946, Huston Cobb Jr. and Sadie Long rekindled their relationship that started during their school days. On October 2, 1947, Huston Cobb Jr. finally married his long-time sweetheart Sadie Long.

Huston and Sadie Long Cobb had two sons and one daughter: Charles Darnell Cobb, Bruce Winford Cobb (deceased), and Cheryl Deresie Cobb. The Huston Cobb Jr. Family picture was taken in front of their 1954 Plymouth at their home on Shaw Road near the home they lived in for many years.

Sadie Long Cobb, Huston Cobb Jr.
Bruce, Cheryl, Darnell

TVA

When Huston Cobb got back from his tour of military duty, he went to the unemployment office seeking work. They give him papers to complete for a government job with TVA. Realizing that he wanted to work at Reynolds Metals instead of TVA, Huston Cobb Jr. tore up his papers as soon as he got out of the unemployment office.

Huston immediately went to Reynolds seeking employment, and he got a job at Reynolds on the same day. Shortly after getting the job at Reynolds, he was laid off work because of a reduction in force.

After being laid off, Huston then went back to farming with his father. He went to apply for farm aid to buy seed and fertilizer, but since he did not answer the questions correctly about share cropping with his father, Huston got nothing.

On November 9, 1942, Huston Cobb Jr. landed a job with TVA. His dad, Houston Cobb Sr., was well recognized and admired by the TVA staff, and he had worked with TVA for over 40 years. Because Houston Sr. was such a good worker, Walter Gholston, a Black personnel manager and officer with TVA, told Huston to take the job no matter what it was. Therefore, Huston Cobb took the job pushing gravel under railroad ties, which was hard work, but he stuck with the job and he was soon promoted.

In 1946, Huston Cobb Jr. bought an International pickup truck from Robert Layton. He swapped the pickup for a two-ton Dodge that belonged to Ed Mauldin. Huston gave $300.00 boot for the big truck; the truck had a door off on the passenger side.

A White man by the name of Earl Percy asked Huston to take his wife to the doctor. When Huston picked the couple up in his truck, Earl sat by Huston and made his wife sit on the seat next to where door was off the truck.

Segregation

Huston said, "We knew things were as bad as they could get for Black and White separation. The TVA cafeteria was set up so the Whites got to use the big room to eat while the Black workers had to use a very small room to eat their meals. There were signs at the cafeteria, restrooms, and water fountains designating and separating use for Whites and Blacks."

"One day when I was getting a drink of water, I inadvertently used the White water fountain; a White worker was standing nearby waiting on a drink. I realized my mistake, and apologized by telling the White man I was sorry. The white man said, 'How do you think I feel.' In other words, he let me know that he did not appreciate me drinking at the White water fountain."

Huston did not get to eat with the White folks until the Peace Corps came to TVA during the mid-1960s. During this time, the Black folks finally got to use the same bathroom, cafeteria, and water fountain as the White people. Huston finally got to go with the Whites to get his food and eat in the main cafeteria.

Eventually, Huston Cobb Jr. was made a foreman, making over $10,000.00 more than the people working under him. Huston said, "For one year, I lived like a White man. My wife and I went on bus tours and saw much of the country. I did it because I was finally financially able to afford a vacation."

After shutting down the phosphorus area at TVA, the supervisor of Huston said he could take a job at the nitric plant, but it would be a cut of $8,000.00 per year in salary. Huston went to the nitric plant but felt like he was starting where he initially begin working for TVA. After hard work and learning all the details of the new job, Huston got to the point he was teaching the new foreman about the details of the job.

After TVA built the coal gasification plant, Huston became foreman after attending school about coal gasification operations. Mr. Willie Long was the plant supervisor. Huston Cobb Jr. eventually became the supervisor over the coal gasification plant. He said, "I never had problem with any Black or White people that worked under me."

Civil Rights

According to Huston Cobb Jr., "We have people who think that the Civil Rights struggle started in the 1960s, but they fail to recognize that people have struggled for a long time for freedom, such as people like Denmark Percy, Nat Turner, Richard Allen, Marcus Kroft, and I could go on and on.

"I remember the Civil Rights Movement very well. I was a Wishful Master in the Masonic Lodge, and I was getting feedback on the activities during the Civil Rights Movement. Alabama Attorney General John Patterson helped shut down the NAACP in 1956, and it was kept shut down until 1965. There was actually not a threat of violence in North Alabama, because Blacks could not carry the majority of votes in this area.

"There was not one Black family that owned a brick house in Sheffield in the 1950s. A Black family could only borrow a maximum of $7,500.00 to build a house, and a brick house could not be built for that price."

Huston Cobb Jr. told about discrimination as follows, "In the early 1950s, Louie Armstrong came to the area, but he could not stay in a hotel because he was Black. One Black family in Sheffield had a brick home, and Louie Armstrong stayed with them. However, years later, I was the first Black juror to be sequestered in a hotel for a trial in the Tuscumbia area."

Huston said, "I turned Republican to know what they are doing. You got to know what is going on in the other room. I ran as a Republican for state representative when Governor Guy Hunt was running on the same platform.

"The late United States Senator Howell Heflin once told me that I was an alright Black person that needs to be in the Republican Party. Who could be better that you Huston Cobb Jr.?"

Huston with former Senator Jeff Sessions

Death of Sadie Long Cobb

Huston Cobb Jr. and his wife, Sadie Long, were married for 50 years. The long-term home of Huston Cobb Jr. and Sadie Long Cobb was on Second Street, or present-day Highway 184, near where his father Houston Cobb Sr. spent the majority of his life. Huston described their former home as an exotic house with lots of glass and a garden in the middle.

Sadie Long Cobb, the lifelong love of Mr. Huston Cobb Jr., passed away on January 18, 1998. She was buried in the Houston Cobb Sr. Family Cemetery in the Bethel Community in Colbert County, Alabama.

Walker Interviews

Besides the intense interviews and historical tours with Mr. Huston Cobb Jr., I interviewed two additional elderly Black men who called northwest Alabama home. These two men were from entirely different backgrounds, but both had stories that built on the foundation of the Black culture and heritage of northwest North Alabama.

Colonel Arthur Graves was a Black man from Tuscumbia who built his fortune with hard work and dedication. He was a career military and businessman with a determination to succeed. Mr. Graves passed those noble attributes along to his children.

While growing up in poverty in the Oakville area of Lawrence County, Alabama, Mr. Charlie Pointer and his brothers became the best baseball players to ever walk on the "Field of Dreams." However, probably because these Black men did not want to leave their homes and families, their dreams of baseball stardom never came to fruition.

Graves, Colonel Arthur D.

The story of Colonel Arthur D. Graves starts with the construction of the Muscle Shoals Canal on the Tennessee River in northwest Alabama during the 1880s. More specifically, the maternal folks of Arthur came from the area of Lake Charles, Louisiana, to Hillsboro in Lawrence County, Alabama.

Edward Doctor Reynolds, the maternal grandfather of Arthur Graves, was the manservant of Captain William Crawford Gorgas. When Gorgas was assigned work on the Muscle Shoals Canal, Edward Reynolds accompanied him to the Tennessee Valley. Edward assisted his boss in the move from Lake Charles to the Muscle Shoals of northwest Alabama, and he brought his Black Creole wife with him.

William Crawford Gorgas

Captain William C. Gorgas worked for the United States Army Corps of Engineers, and he moved from Lake Charles to assist with the canal being built through the Muscle Shoals in the Tennessee River. Gorgas had accepted an assignment of helping complete the Muscle Shoals Canal near Browns Ferry in Lawrence County, Alabama, and Edward D. Reynolds came with his employer.

Major General William Crawford Gorgas
10/3/1854–7/3/1920

Bridges across the Tennessee River were not in existence and work on the Muscle Shoals Canal had begun under the leadership of George Washington Goethals. Therefore, Captain Gorgas was put in charge of the river crossing and controlling mosquitoes that were causing outbreaks of yellow fever and malaria.

Captain Gorgas was chief engineer in charge of the operation of the Tennessee River crossing at Browns Ferry. Browns Ferry was located at the head of the Muscle Shoals Canal, and it was located just east of the upstream beginning of Elk River Shoals. The ferry was maintained to insure that people were able to cross the river throughout the year.

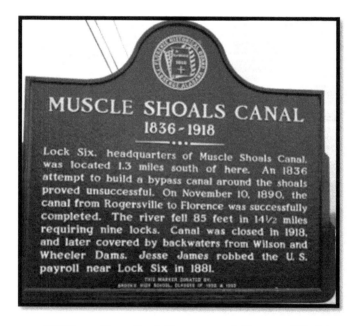

MUSCLE SHOALS CANAL
1836-1918

Lock Six, headquarters of Muscle Shoals Canal, was located 1.3 miles south of here. An 1836 attempt to build a bypass canal around the shoals proved unsuccessful. On November 10, 1890, the canal from Rogersville to Florence was successfully completed. The river fell 85 feet in 14½ miles requiring nine locks. Canal was closed in 1918, and later covered by backwaters from Wilson and Wheeler Dams. Jesse James robbed the U.S. payroll near Lock Six in 1881.

William Crawford Gorgas and George Washington Goethals were assigned duty at the engineering camp headquarters on the Muscle Shoals Canal near Melton's Bluff in Lawrence County, Alabama. George Washington

Goethals had the engineering knowledge to build and complete the canal through the Muscle Shoals of the Tennessee River, and Gorgas, who early in life had contracted yellow fever that was carried by mosquitoes, had the medical knowledge to eradicate breeding areas of mosquitoes to control yellow fever and malaria. Both these great men were initially assigned to the complete the Muscle Shoals Canal.

After being successful in North Alabama, both Gorgas and Goethals were assigned the task of completing the Panama Canal from the Atlantic Ocean to the Pacific Ocean. Their combined efforts were successful in the completion of the Panama Canal in the Central American country of Panama.

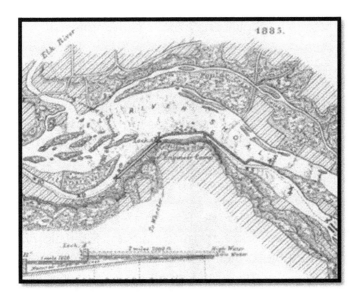

Edward Doctor Reynolds

Edward D. Reynolds was a redheaded Irishman

who had married a Black Creole lady by the name of Adeline McEntyre Reynolds from Lake Charles, Louisiana. Reynolds and his family made their home in the Hillsboro Community of Lawrence County, Alabama.

When Captain Gorgas was assigned duty at the Panama Canal after successfully completing the Muscle Shoals Canal, Reynolds stayed at Hillsboro. Edward continued to run the store that he had established in the small town of Hillsboro.

While living in Lawrence County, Alabama, Edward D. Reynolds and his wife Adeline received from the Civil War Reconstruction a temporary deed for 40 acres and two mules. Edward used the mules to cultivate the land and plant crops. He and his wife had to farm the land for two years before they could receive title to the property.

After a few years, Edward D. Reynolds opened a general store where the old Hillsboro Road crossed the Southern Railroad. He maintained accurate records on credit that he had given to the local farmers in order to make a crop. During the tough economic times and bad crops, a lot of farmers were unable to pay their bills owed to Edward D. Reynolds

During the tough farming years, many of the landowners that owed Reynolds money for their failed crops left the area; therefore, Reynolds foreclosed on the farmers and took their land because of delinquent credit. Reynolds wound up acquiring their property, which eventually accumulated to some 2,600 acres of land in the area of Hillsboro, Alabama.

Not only did Reynolds maintain a store, but he also built a cotton gin that operated until the 1930s. He also had a grist mill and the first Coca-Cola Bottling Company at Hillsboro, which was the first of its kind in North Alabama.

Edward D. Reynolds was a dedicated owner and worker in his general store. He stayed in the store building 24 hours a day for six days. Reynolds would go home on Saturday afternoon, and he would return to his store on Sunday evening. He stayed in the store to protect his financial interests. Just one block from his store, Reynolds owned a huge two-storied house that had indoor toilets and electricity powered by a two-cylinder engine.

Reynolds and his wife had seven girls and six boys who were half-Irish and half-Black Creole; all their children married Black individuals. The girls were Alice, Mattie, Addie, Clara, Carrie, Anabelle, and Odell, and the boys were Richard, Edward, Clarence, George, John, and one son that died as an infant. Alice and Richard were the only Reynolds children that were born in Lake Charles, Louisiana; the rest were born in Hillsboro in Lawrence County, Alabama.

The Reynolds children had complete access to the store, and they could come and go as they pleased. The children were not allowed to spend the night away from home.

The Reynolds children were sent to some of the best schools in the area. Edward Reynolds sent his children to Huntsville, Atlanta, or Nashville to get the best schooling that he could find for his children.

After Edward Doctor Reynolds died, some 2,600 acres of land and his possessions were split between his thirteen children. Reynolds had moved from a poor manservant of the young Captain William C. Gorgas to become one of the wealthiest men in the Hillsboro area of North Alabama.

Alice Reynolds and Frank Graves

The oldest child of Edward D. Reynolds and Adeline McEntyre Reynolds was Alice, who was born in Lake Charles, Louisiana. Alice Reynolds assisted her dad in the store, and she kept up with running the business for her father. After completing high school, Alice was sent to Alabama A&M University, where she received a college education.

After graduating from college, Alice taught public school for a short period in Moulton, Alabama in 1898. Alice Reynolds became one of the first registered Black female voters in 1921. Her son, Arthur Graves, still cherishes her voter registration certificate.

Alice Reynolds married Frank Graves, a Black fireman who supplied coal to the boiler on the steam engine of the Southern Railroad train engine. Frank Graves was a native of Tyler, Texas, and hoboed from Texas to Memphis, Tennessee. Frank eventually settled in Tuscumbia, Alabama, after he and Alice were married.

Frank worked for the Southern Railroad all his working career. The train would leave Memphis and had stops in Tuscumbia and Sheffield. The train engine turned around in Sheffield and another engine would work from Sheffield to Chattanooga, Tennessee. Since Frank was working for the railroad during the depression, the Graves family did not suffer due to the difficult times.

During the Great Depression, every vacant lot around the Graves home in Tuscumbia was planted by the family. They raised hogs and chickens. The family also had a large garden of vegetables such as beans, corn, sweet potatoes, greens, and other vegetables, and they had sugar cane which was processed by Mr. Leo Merritt for a share of the molasses.

In other words, during the Great Depression, the Graves family was not rich, but they did not go hungry and had plenty of food that they would sometimes share with strangers whether they were Black or White. Arthur Graves said, "I really do not know about the depression because I always had a roof over my head, two mules in the barn, pens of chickens, and killed hogs for meat."

Even though Frank never owned a car, he could tell you how fast an automobile was traveling by counting the telephone posts. He had been so accustomed to counting the posts along the rail lines, knowing the speed of a vehicle was very simple matter of the intervals between the power poles. He could not write, but Frank was far from being ignorant, and he was a very intelligent man.

Frank and Alice Reynolds Graves had seven children, all of whom graduated from college. Their children were Patsy, Frank, Alice, Isaac, John, Arthur, and Gloria.

Frank required his children to sit at the table with the whole family to have dinner. Frank and Alice were very family oriented; they required that the children were seated and present at the table during the family meals. Both Frank and Alice had very high expectations for their children, and they pushed their children to be successful people in society. Both Frank Graves and his wife Alice Reynolds Graves passed away in the late 1980s.

Colonel Arthur Graves

On February 7, 1927, Arthur Graves was born in the two-story frame home of his parents in Tuscumbia, Alabama. The spacious house had indoor toilets and four bedrooms. As an adult, Arthur lived in a fine brick home at the very location where he was born.

Arthur Graves and Rickey Butch Walker

One day when Arthur was a small boy, he noticed a large crowd gathered at the home of Mr. Percy Ricks, who was his next-door neighbor at 802 East Eighth Street in

Tuscumbia. Arthur went over to the Ricks home and saw Walter Jackson, C. E. Lesley, and a large group of people surrounding one of the most famous Black men of his time, Dr. George Washington Carver.

As Arthur tried to get closer to Dr. Carver, he bumped into a small evergreen bush that contained a large wasp nest. The wasps became stirred up and one stung Arthur. Everyone scattered except Dr. Carver who came to the rescue of Arthur. Carver grabbed leaves from three different trees, and he twisted the leaves together and rubbed them on Arthur's wasp sting. Arthur said immediately the pain of the sting left, and he did not have any swelling.

Later that evening, Arthur went to Sheffield High School to listen to a speech given by Dr. George Washington Carver. Arthur had to sit in the balcony because Black folks were not allowed to sit with the White folks.

Arthur also related that most of the wealthy White folks used Black wet nurses to breastfeed their infants. The White folks would not allow a White wet nurse to breast feed their babies because they felt the baby would become attached to a White wet nurse. Wet nurses would also chew the food prior to feeding it to the baby. The nurses would take small portions of beef, pork, mutton, fruit, or vegetables to chew until soft before feeding it to the babies. The Black wet nurses who attended White churches to take care of babies had to sit in the balcony of the church because they were not allowed to sit with the White folks; however, it was warmer in the wintertime due to the rising heat.

When Arthur Graves was a young boy, he had to lead the cow and mule to the pasture, and he walked past the big home that had been built by George Lawrence. When he was small, Arthur played with Lawrence's daughters Susie Bitting Lawrence and Martha Frances Lawrence.

While in high school, Arthur worked for George Lawrence's car business. Mr. Lawrence agreed to sell Arthur a car for one dollar per week. Arthur was real excited to buy a car, but he decided that he should first talk to his father before bringing the car home. Even though he was happy to get a car, Arthur knew that he had to discuss the deal with his father, Frank Graves.

Arthur was surprised when his father asked him, "Where are you going to park this car?" Arthur said, "Since you do not have a car, I will park it in the driveway." Frank replied, "You do not have a driveway! My advice to you is do not buy anything until you have a place to put it; therefore, you cannot put that car in my driveway."

After the discussion with his father, Arthur Graves decided the best thing for him to do was to go to college. Since his brothers were at Tuskegee, Arthur enrolled in school where his brothers were attending. After some time in college, Arthur decided to come home in November and go back to work for Mr. Lawrence, who eventually sold the dealership in 1946 or 1947.

One night in March, Arthur came home at three in the morning, and his father was up waiting on him to get home. His dad Frank told him, "Arthur you have been home since returning from Tuskegee, and I expected you to start paying rent since you are working and coming home at all hours. If you stay here, you will pay me room and board of ten dollars per week."

Immediately, Arthur went upstairs and packed his bags. At five that morning, Arthur took his suitcases, and he left home that March morning. He headed back to Tuskegee to complete his college degree. At Tuskegee, Arthur got in a work-study program, washed cars, and worked odd jobs to earn money for his school expenses.

Arthur stayed at Tuskegee until he was drafted in May 1946, and he was sent to Sheppard Air Force Base in Wichita Falls, Texas. He became a drill instructor, and he was a clerk in the orderly room.

Since the atomic bomb was dropped on Hiroshima, Japan, and the war ended shortly thereafter, Arthur served only eight months and 29 days before returning to Tuskegee, Alabama, where he reenrolled in college. Arthur graduated from Tuskegee University in 1948.

At his graduation ceremony, Arthur's brother drove his father Frank and mother Alice to the see their son get his degree. From Tuskegee, his parents and brother drove to Washington, D.C. to see his baby sister, Gloria Graves, graduate from college. Eventually, all of the Graves children graduated from college.

In 1949, Arthur Graves got a job teaching in the public schools in Decatur, Alabama. While in the Decatur public schools, he got called back to active duty during the Korean War. Even though Arthur did not have to go to Korea, he served on active duty for a total of 20 years in the armed forces.

Initially, he was a drill instructor of Black troops. At the time Arthur served as a drill instructor, the military had just begun to use Black instructors. President Truman had desegregated all the services around 1948, but the order did not desegregate the people.

While on active duty, Arthur Graves acquired the rank of Colonel. Even though the military services were officially integrated, Black troops still had to endure the racial overtones of other White military leaders. Colonel Arthur Graves referred to these people as ring knockers because of their West Point rings.

Graves said, "From the time of the baseball great Jackie Robinson and General B.O. Davis with the Tuskegee Airmen, one thing that sustained the Black troops was the attitude to be successful. The old attitudes had problems with life itself and were hard to change, but at first most military people were not willing to accept change; Blacks in the military still run into segregation issues."

Arthur Graves stayed sick during his flight training in the air corps. He was later diagnosed with severe anxiety because of the fear of flying. Arthur said he did not have a problem while in the air but before a flight he always got sick. He was in advanced training for flying B-25s in the Old Army Air Corps.

After serving over 20 years, Colonel Arthur Graves retired from the United States military and began teaching. On December 31, 1974, he started as a college professor at the University of North Alabama. He taught for 14 years before retiring from the college in 1988.

Arthur Graves eventually became the executor of the estate of his deceased uncle who had inherited about

400 acres of his grandfather's estate. His uncle had also purchased additional property when many farmers went under during the depression. Arthur's uncle had a bright redheaded son who became an alcoholic and wrote many bad checks for which he was incarcerated in the local jail.

Judge Vanderhoff stated that the boy was his own worst enemy, and he placed Arthur Graves over his estate to manage. Arthur sold off some of the land to pay off the bad checks, provide for his cousin, and keep him out of jail. Arthur eventually sold all the land around Hillsboro, Alabama, that belonged to his Reynolds uncle.

Arthur and Jean Long Graves

On November 22, 1958, Arthur Graves married Jean Long of Colbert County, Alabama. They had been married for 53 years when I interviewed Mr. Graves.

The father of Jean Long Graves was William Mansel Long, who was from Lane Springs in northwest Colbert County. Her mother was Otelia Mullins, who was from the Ricks Community near The Oaks Plantation which was also in Colbert County. Otelia was probably a descendant of the Black slaves of the White Mullins Family, who had 43 Black slaves according to the 1830 Franklin County, Alabama, census records.

Arthur and Jean Graves had three children: Lisa Graves Minor graduated from Vanderbilt University, Kenneth Graves graduated from Cumberland Law School, and Sherry Graves Smith graduated from the University of Alabama and Cumberland Law School.

Arthur had two children from a previous marriage. Of his sons, Arthur B. Graves is a retired educator, and Frank Graves is a retired dentist.

In 1982, Arthur Graves bought and paid for a funeral home from Ms. Eloise Thompson that he operated for years. Graves said, "I have had a radio program for 25 years. The radio program costs me $800.00 per month, and I am on the air on Sunday starting at 9:15 a.m. to promote my funeral home business. I go to the Methodist Church, and the rest of my family goes to the Church of Christ.

"I believe one of our greatest rights is the freedom to vote. I am a member of the 47% and draw three retirements! I will work as long as God blesses me and my good health."

Biography of Arthur Graves

The following was the biography of Colonel Arthur D. Graves from the Colbert County Historical Landmarks Foundation:

"U.S. Air Force Lt. Colonel Arthur D. Graves will be the guest speaker. His Black History Month presentation will cover the three basic structures (the family, church and schools) that African Americans relied upon as social support systems that aided them to 'go from the out-house to the White House.'

Colonel Graves, a World War II veteran, received his AFROTC commission from Tuskegee Institute in 1949 and entered active service in 1951; serving at Hondo AFB, Texas; Reese AFB, Texas; Laredo AFB, Texas; Maxwell AFB, Montgomery, AL; Brookley AFB, Mobile; Eglin

AFB, Florida; Moulin's AFB, France; Daharan AFB, Saudia Arabia; Clark AFB, Philippine Islands; and Southern Command Headquarters in the Panama Canal Zone.

Lt. Col. Graves is a graduate of Trenholm High School, and Tuskegee University. He earned a Master's degree from Tennessee State University and Education Specialist Degree from the University of North Alabama.

In 1949, he began his teaching career as a public school teacher at the Old Courtland Colored High School. Serving there a year, he later taught at Decatur High School for a year. While living in Lawrence County, he began working for his uncle, Mr. George Reynolds, at Reynolds Funeral Home in Decatur, Alabama. He then entered the United States Air Force and remained in service for twenty years. He is owner and operator of Thompson & Sons Funeral Home in Tuscumbia.

Married to Mrs. Jean Long Graves, they are the parents of three children: Dr. Lisa Graves Minor (Julian), Professor of English at the University of North Alabama; Attorney Kenneth D. Graves (Tamekia), Chief Legal Officer for Huntsville Hospital; and Attorney Sherri Graves-Smith (William), Legal Counselor at Coca-Cola Headquarters in Atlanta, GA, and two granddaughters: Leslie Minor and Kristen Graves."

Pointer, Charlie

On a visit to his home on January 31, 2013, Charlie Pointer told me that he turned 89 years old on January 1, 2013. He said, "I had a stroke not long ago, but it did not hurt my mind; the people at the nursing home have helped me recover a lot of use of my right arm and hand. I have always lived within five miles of where I was born." Even though Charlie was hard of hearing, his mind was sharp as a tack. He immediately started telling me

Charlie Pointer

of his boyhood days like it was yesterday.

Charlie knew that I had talked to him on several occasions, and he knew I wanted him to tell me the history of his family. He began telling me about the struggles for survival when times for Black folks were nearly as bad as the days of slavery. He told me of his dad making ten cents per day for long days of labor.

If his parents did not do the work that the landowner required, they would have to find another place to live. Sometimes Charlie's folks were not paid a dime for their hard farm work, but they were given a ticket that could be swapped at the store for food. Charlie grew up in a time that was tough to even survive; wages were extremely low, the work was extremely hard, the days were long, but his family had to have a home.

From his chair in the living room of his home, Charlie pointed south toward West Flint Creek which lay just south of the Old Moulton Road. He said, "I was born just across West Flint Creek on the Lamar Cartwright place on January 1, 1924." Charlie's present-day home is approximately one mile north of Red Hill Cemetery, which is adjacent to the Old Moulton Road; the cemetery is a few miles west of the present-day Five Points Store.

Jim Pointer and Mattie Griffin

Charlie's father was Jackson Pointer; Jackson's parents were Jim Pointer and Mattie (Matt) Griffin. Matt Griffin Pointer was 104 years old when she died. Mattie was buried in the old Lindsey Cemetery just east of the present-day Jesse Owens Park.

Charlie said that his grandfather, Jim Pointer, came from a cotton plantation near the Tennessee River in northeast Lawrence County where he was born a slave. In 1830, Thomas M. Pointer was the first member of the White Pointer Family to be listed in Lawrence Alabama; at that time, Thomas was listed as owning 30 Black slaves. Thomas also owned some 860 acres of cotton land near the drainage of Mallard Creek at Elk River Shoals on the Tennessee River.

When Jim Pointer was a young man just after the Civil War, he walked from the area near the Tennessee River to Alexander Plantation south of Oakville and settled in the Pinhook area. Jim was getting away from the area and the White cotton planters that had enslaved his folks for generations.

At the Alexander Plantation, Charlie said that Jim Pointer met and married his wife, Mattie (Matt) Griffin, who was born a Black slave. The Black Griffin Family probably got their family name from a White cotton planter and slave owner by the name of G. W. Griffin. Mattie Griffin may have been kinfolks to Mack Griffin of Moulton, who was the great-grandfather of Huston Cobb Jr.

Mattie Griffin lived on the Alexander Plantation where she met Jim Pointer. Sometime just after the Civil War, Jim and Mattie married; initially, they lived and worked on the Alexander Plantation.

The overseer of the former slaves and post-Civil War farmhands for the Alexander Plantation was William Todd Kelsoe. During the time of Thomas Jefferson Alexander and later Jake Alexander, William Todd Kelsoe became known as "Boss." He was in charge of the White and Black farmhands that lived and worked on the Alexander Plantation. The wife of Boss Kelsoe was Mary Teague, a Cherokee Indian.

Alexander Plantation

Jim Pointer worked for a while on the Alexander Plantation located on the north edge of the Black Warrior Mountains of Lawrence County. Initially, the Alexander Plantation contained some 10,000 acres in the early days of the county, before the land was divided among the Alexander heirs. The original owner of the cotton plantation was James Alexander.

James Alexander first married Kitty Walker, who was born in 1782 in North Carolina; she died on May 5, 1823. Kitty was thought to be kin to my fourth-great-grandfather, William Walker. He was born in 1762, and his son William Walker Jr. was born in 1790 in Mecklenburg

County, North Carolina. James and Kitty Walker Alexander are buried in the Old Alexander Cemetery, which is about 100 yards north of where my parents are buried.

Later, William Alexander and his wife, Mary Aldridge Alexander, owned the plantation. William Alexander, son of James and Kitty, was born on November 20, 1803, and he died on April 4, 1873. William married Mary Aldridge on May 15, 1823; Mary was born on December 22, 1802, in Abbeville, South Carolina.

According to family members, William Alexander could ride his horse from Danville to Wren and never get off his land. William and Mary are buried in the Alexander-Welborn Cemetery near Pinhook Community.

According to family history, William Alexander owned some 32 Black slaves that became the property of Thomas Jefferson Alexander. After the Civil War, several of the former Black slaves continued to work for Thomas Jefferson Alexander.

Thomas Jefferson Alexander, son of William and Mary, was born on August 7, 1835, and he died August 30, 1890. Thomas Jefferson Alexander was the grandson of James and Kitty Walker Alexander, who are buried in the Pinhook Community.

Thomas Jefferson Alexander was said to have fathered several children by Black women. Many of the Black Alexanders in Moulton, Alabama, claim kinship to the White Alexander folks through Thomas Jefferson Alexander. In addition, the Fitzgeralds of the Oakville area also claim kinship to the White Alexanders thorough Thomas Jefferson Alexander.

117

The first wife of Thomas Jefferson Alexander was Caroline Warren. When Caroline got sick and bedfast, Thomas brought a young White woman by the name of Sallie Fitzgerald to help take care of Ms. Caroline.

Evidently, Sallie got pregnant by Thomas Jefferson Alexander, and she was asked to leave the home. Two years later, Caroline Warren Alexander died, and Thomas Jefferson Alexander moved Sallie and his two-year-old son Jake back into the Alexander Plantation home.

When Ms. Sallie moved back into the house, she brought a Black house maid with her to take care of the home. According to the late Marvin Fitzgerald, a Black man from Oakville, "The Black housekeeper of Sallie Fitzgerald got pregnant by Thomas Jefferson Alexander, and that was how I and other Black Fitzgeralds were related to the White Alexander family."

Alexander Plantation House

While on the Alexander Plantation, Jim farmed and helped make bricks; the Alexander farm had a large brick kiln that was operated by Black farmhands who kept the fire going continuously day and night until the bricks were hardened. Many of the handmade bricks were used to make chimneys on the Alexander, Preuit, Willis, Warren, and other places in the area.

Charlie Pointer said, "My grandmother was Mattie 'Matt' Griffin, and she was born a slave. Some of her folks were Black slaves to the Alexander Plantation. That was where my grandparents Jim and Matt met each other."

Charlie said, "My grandmother Matt told many stories about the Yankees coming through the area during the Civil War. She said that folks took their belongings, cows, mules, and other things to a large bluff shelter in the mountains where they were hid until the Union soldiers would leave the plantation. Matt told my family that the bluff shelter was large enough to put an average house under that overhanging rock. Sometimes they would also carry their belongings in wagons into Indian Tomb Hollow to avoid the Union troops that were coming through the area destroying everything they could find. Many folks on the Alexander Plantation would herd their hogs, mules, cattle, and horses into the Sugar Camp Hollow to hide them from the Yankee soldiers."

Pointer, McDaniel, and Elliott Slaves

The Black Pointer Family were descendants of the 104 Black slaves listed in 1850 census of the White Pointer Family of Lawrence County, Alabama. According to the 1850 census, the Black slaves belonged to Phillip Pointer with 39, William R. Pointer with 24, Sarah Pointer with 22, and Thomas M. Pointer with 19.

In 1860, M. A. Pointer was listed as being a female who was 58 years old from Virginia. Her occupation was farming, and she had 19 Black slaves. She probably inherited her slaves from Thomas M. Pointer, who had the same number in 1850. Also in 1860, Samuel Pointer had 22 slaves, which is the same amount that Sarah Pointer had in 1850; not sure if there was a relationship between Samuel and Sarah Pointer.

In 1850, Phillip Pointer is listed as being 44 years of age from Virginia; Sarah, age 32 from Virginia; Thomas S., age 11, born in Alabama; Mary A., age eight; Phillip Jr., age nine; Emma L., age six; Martha A.(Patsy), age three; and, John, age one. In 1860, Phillip Pointer was not listed in the census, but his estate was listed as having eight heirs and 44 Black slaves; between 1850 and 1860, Phillip gained five slaves. Phillip Sr. had another child in 1853 who is listed as Phlem, a son of seven years old born in Alabama.

The Black McDaniel Family that intermarried into the Black Pointer Family were probably descendants from the slaves of two White men—either P. A. McDaniel or Thomas McDaniel. According to the 1860 slave census, P. A. McDaniel owned 67 Black slaves and Thomas McDaniel owned 59 Black slaves.

The McDaniel Mill was located on the West Fork of Flint Creek about three or four miles from the present-day Jesse Owens Park in Oakville. Many of the older White members of the McDaniel Family were buried in Oakville within a few yards southwest of the P. B. Lowery home. The cemetery was behind the old P. B. Lowery barn, and tombstones have been disturbed. The old McDaniel Cemetery on the P. B. Lowery property is only a quarter mile north of the present-day Jesse Owens Park and a few hundred yards east of the Oakville Indian Mounds Park and Museum.

The Elliott Family member that intermarried with Black Pointer Family was probably a descendant of the 94 black slaves listed in the 1860 slave census as being owned by Samuel Elliott of Lawrence County, Alabama. According to the 1860 census, Samuel Elliott was a planter listed as being 49 years old from Tennessee; Elizabeth P., age 37, was from Alabama; Leonidas, age 24, male; Mary F., age 17, Jerimiah, age 12; Randolph, age 10; Catherine, age three; Ann P., three months; Mary Green, age 25, school mistress; Andrew Woldridge, age 24, Tennessee, Methodist clergyman; and Sarah E., age 21, Tennessee.

The Black Elliott Family may have been the slaves of William Elliott, who was listed in the 1820 Census of Lawrence County, Alabama, as having 12 slaves. In the 1860 census, William Elliott (Ellitt or Ellett) was listed as being 58 years old from Virginia and owning 19 Black slaves.

Jackson and Lucy Taylor Pointer

At the time that Jackson "Jack" Pointer was born on the Alexander Plantation in 1891, Jake Alexander was in charge of the plantation. The Alexander Plantation had passed to Jake from Thomas Jefferson Alexander (8/7/1835–8/3/1890); the place was passed to Thomas from William Alexander (11/20/1803–4/4/1873), and it was passed to William from James Alexander (1770–8/26/1851).

The father of Charlie Pointer was Jackson "Jack" Pointer and his mother was Lucy Taylor. On April 4, 1911, Jack and Lucy were married; they had seven children:

1. Corene Pointer, who married Son Hill.
2. Ruth Pointer, who never married.
3. Robert Pointer, who got shot and killed with a rifle by Ab Rogers; Rogers was sent to the penitentiary.
4. Louie Pointer, who married Lilly McDaniel.
5. Dee Pointer, who married Geneva, the daughter of Lizzie Ann McDaniel (Po Duck).
6. Aaron Pointer, who married Hoyl Elliott.
7. Charlie Pointer, who married Louise Price.

Jackson (Jack) Pointer lived and worked on the old Alexander Plantation until he was around twelve years old. When Jack was real young, he helped Ben Price and other Black folks make bricks on the Alexander place. There were brick kilns southwest of the Alexander home near the limestone glade that was run by Black folks.

Later, Jack started working and farming the cotton fields for the Jacobs Family near the store of Mr. Will Melson. When I, Rickey Butch Walker, was a little boy, I remember going with my folks to Mr. Will Melson's store. It was scary watching Mr. Melson cut slices off those huge rounds sticks of bologna with a big butcher knife. The bologna sticks were four to six inches across, and one slice made a great sandwich.

Charlie Pointer said, "Will Melson had a record of my dad's birth. He kept that record in their old Melson Family Bible."

Ms. Mildred Brackin Lee said, "Uncle Jackson Pointer was the hardest working man that I ever knew. He was small in size and not very tall, but he would work you to death. Uncle Jack was always far out front of everybody chopping cotton."

Mildred said, "One day my cousin Aaron Pointer was going to out-chop his dad Uncle Jack Pointer. Aaron started chopping cotton as fast as he could and tried to get in front of his dad. When they got to the end of the row, Uncle Jack did not slow down. He started another row, and Aaron was close on his heels. Finally, Aaron caught up to his dad and brushed his heel with the hoe. Uncle Jack stopped, and after a few choice words, Aaron knew better than to get close to his dad again."

Mildred continued, "Everyone laughed at the situation and Uncle Jack hollered, 'What are y'all laughing at' and went right back to chopping cotton as hard as he could. But it did not matter how hard Uncle Jack and our family worked, we never got out of debt with the landowner. They would always say, 'maybe you can get out of debt next year,' but it never happened."

After working for the Jacobs, Jack moved to the Lamar Cartwright place on the West Fork of Flint Creek just north of the Old Moulton Road in the Red Hill Community, which is a few miles north of Oakville. Charlie said, "I was born on the Cartwright place. When I was a small boy, most of the place was covered in forest land and contained huge stands of timber. My dad Jack and my older brothers began clearing the trees and turning much of the timber land into pastures and row crops."

Jackson Pointer worked for Cartwright for several years. Charlie was too young to help his dad cut timber and make new grounds for row crops on the Cartwright place. But even as a small boy, Charlie was responsible for making sure that his father and older brothers had plenty of water to drink while they were clearing the woodlands. Charlie said, "I kept busy toting water to the men cutting the trees on the Cartwright place. Even though I was a small boy, I would take drinking water to my daddy and older brothers. Just about the whole place was covered in big trees and we cleared the land so they could plant crops."

The parents of Lucy Taylor were Joe and Rachel Taylor who lived in Moulton, Alabama. Joe had a brother by the name of Amos Taylor who owned a big farm and ran a store in Moulton.

Charlie remembers walking with his mother, Lucy, to Uncle Amos Taylor's place. He said, "Uncle Amos was always dressed up and wore a suit and tie."

Charlie also remembered that Lucy's brother, Jerry Taylor, made whiskey and was eventually caught. Charlie said, "Uncle Jerry was sent to the penitentiary. The law said that they did not want him to come back to Lawrence County. My Uncle Jerry was killed in prison."

Charlie said, "My Uncle James (Sonny) Taylor got killed playing his favorite game, which was rolling dice. Gambling was not only fun to Uncle Sonny, but it was also a way he made a lot of money. My Uncle Sonny kept the people broke who rolled dice with him. Sonny kept a pistol with him all the time, and many times, just liked to threatened people with his gun."

Charlie continued, "One particular day, Uncle Sonny Taylor and a White man by the last name of Lindsey were rolling dice. Lindsey felt he had been cheated and slipped up behind Sonny with a butcher knife. When Sonny reached to pick up the dice that he had just rolled, Lindsey cut his throat from ear to ear. Uncle Sonny Taylor was able to get his pistol and get off two shots before he died, but the bullets did not hit anyone."

Jackson Pointer moved to the Preuit Farm

Charlie Pointer's father and older brothers were the Black farmhands for Lamar Cartwright. The place Cartwright was on the West Fork of Flint Creek near Five Points Community.

In the late 1920s, Jackson moved his family to the Clebe Preuit farm when Charlie was about six years old. Charlie said, "My grandparents, Jim and Matt Pointer, had earlier worked for the Preuit Family years before my dad started working for them."

The Black Pointer Family moved from the Cartwright place to a little frame house located in the northeast corner of Lawrence County Highway 212 and Lawrence County Highway 211 on the old Preuit Farm. The old home site of the family of Charlie Pointer was less than a quarter mile west of the present home of Rickey Butch Walker, the author of this book.

The little plank house that the Jackson Pointer Family moved in was located on an old Indian trail known as the Coosa Path or Muscle Shoals Path. The Indian path came from Chickasaw Island, just east of Ditto's Landing south of Huntsville, Alabama. The route passed through Hartselle, then Danville, to Oakville, by the Preuit Farm, then Moulton, and to Tuscumbia Landing in Colbert County, circumventing the rough and rugged rapids of the Tennessee River. The Indian path passed south of the Elk River Shoals, Big Muscle Shoals, and Little Muscle Shoals. This particular section of the Tennessee River was very dangerous and treacherous to boat travel. Today, the portion of the Indian trail that passes the Preuit home place is Lawrence County Road 211.

White Family of Preuits

The Preuit Family originally came to America from Scotland in 1687, and they first settled in Virginia. The Preuits were connected through intermarriage to the Cartwright Family. Two of the sisters of Clebe Preuit married two Cartwright boys.

When Charlie was a little boy, his father Jackson Pointer and his brothers started doing farm work for Patrick Cleburn (Clebe) Preuit. The parents of Clebe were John William Preuit (August 8, 1834–August 19, 1923) and Martha E. McDaniel Preuit (August 13, 1839– September 20, 1907). Martha was the daughter of P. A. McDaniel and Ann Leeper.

Martha (Mattie) Eleanor McDaniel Preuit

According to the 1860 Lawrence County, Alabama Census, P. A McDaniel owned 67

Black slaves. Many of the Black folks in Lawrence County, Alabama, by the name of McDaniel and Preuit are probably the descendants of the slaves of the White McDaniel and Preuit families.

John William and Martha McDaniel Preuit had ten children born in Lawrence County, Alabama: Cora Ann Preuit, who married Peter Edward Cartwright on January 1, 1879; Travis Lamar Preuit (1860–1892); Vashti A. A. Preuit (1862–1867); Thelma Blanche Preuit, who married Dr. Oscar Bradley Cartwright; Sallie Octavia Preuit, who married R. T. Burleson and S. R. Martin; John William Preuit Jr., who died in infancy; Patrick Cleburn (Clebe) Preuit; Brent Elmo Preuit, who married Maud Brackins and Elizabeth Brown; Jacob Jackson Preuit; and Minnie Preuit, who married Thomas Durrett Simms.

John William Preuit was listed in the 1850 census slave schedules as having 22 Black slaves, and his wife, Martha McDaniel Preuit, was listed as having 43 Black slaves.

John William Preuit 1921

Today, the home of Rickey Butch Walker is on the original site of the John William and Martha Preuit home. John and Martha are buried in the little Preuit Cemetery which is on my property and located behind my house on Highway 211.

John William Preuit inherited the place from his parents, William Madison Preuit and Martha Looney, who

127

purchased the property from the Robert Price Family in 1825. William Madison and Martha Looney Preuit lived in the original house that was built prior to 1815, which was before the Indian lands were taken by the Turkey Town Treaty of September 1816.

The original log cabin built on Cherokee Indian land was the dwelling place of Cherokees who occupied the area until the treaty was ratified by Congress in July 1817. Nearby Oakville was a Cherokee trading village and hosted a number of Indian people in the surrounding area. Some say that Robert Price added to the Indian cabin; the addition to the house was built on Cherokee land prior to the Indians ceding their territory.

The original house was a two-room log cabin separated by a dogtrot. After William Madison Preuit and Martha Looney Preuit moved from Madison County to the place in 1825, four additional rooms were added to the house which included two upstairs and two behind the original Cherokee cabin. In addition, the logs were covered on the outside with plank board siding and ceilings were added to the log rooms.

Since the Preuits owned some 65 Black slaves, most of the home construction and remodeling was done by their servants and farmhands. The bricks were made by the Black slaves owned by the family; brick chimneys were built on both sides of the house. Brick fireplaces provided heat to the upstairs and downstairs rooms. The fireplace mantles were hand carved by the grandfather of Finis and Walter Bass. The front yard of the house was also covered with slave-made bricks and a picket fence was built around the yard.

During the occupation of the home by the Preuit Family, some 35 members of the Preuits were born in the house. Several generations were born in the house: John William Preuit, the son of William Madison Preuit; Patrick Cleburn Preuit, the son of John William Preuit; John Hodges Preuit, the son of John William Preuit; and Ward Preuit, the son of John Hodges Preuit, was the last member of the family to be born in the house.

In February 1959, the original plank-covered log house was torn down after standing about 145 years to make room for a new house which was built on the same location. John H. Preuit built a new brick house in the early 1960s. He also built a detached garage made from the old slave bricks in the chimneys of the original home.

Ward and John Preuit at Preuit Home 1959

The Black family of Mr. Tom Stover were the last sharecropper folks to live in the original Preuit plantation home. This Black family sharecropped for the Preuits for several years. According to Mr. John Stover, "I was raised up on the Preuit place. Where your (Rickey Butch Walker) house sits, there used to be an old two-story house where my Granddaddy Tom Stover lived there many years. Matter of fact, he lived there until it was torn down, and Mr. John Preuit built a house there."

John Stover continued, "Between 1946 and 1958, my father lived there also. It was an old plantation house, two-story, two-family house with a hallway in between. On one side, there were three rooms downstairs and a pantry, and the other side was one room upstairs and two rooms downstairs."

John said, "I was told that there was a cemetery for Black slaves by some cedar trees out there, but no sign of burial markers. There were seven sharecropper houses on the property that I know of. I learned to milk a cow in the old three-story barn."

I, Rickey Butch Walker, purchased the home in September 2003. The John Preuit House that I bought from Ward Preuit's son, Johnny, was destroyed by a tornado on February 6, 2008. I rebuilt another house on the same foundation and completed the new home on March 11, 2009. I gave most of the slave brick to my sister, Diane Walker Thrasher.

Streight's Raid

During the Civil War on April 29, 1863, Union Colonel Able Streight and some 1,500 Yankee cavalrymen passed by the Preuit place. Streight was chased by Confederate General Nathan Bedford Forrest with his command of some 500 cavalry soldiers. This particular Union action through the area was referred to as Streight's Raid.

Three Union soldiers died on the Preuit Farm during the Civil War, and one was buried in the cemetery behind my house. The Union soldier buried on my property has a marker that reads unknown. The other two Union soldiers are buried on the Preuit place just west of Highway 212 near the present-day home of Willie Hood. Supposedly, the Preuit slaves buried the Union soldiers. Several Rebel and Yankee troops passed along the road that ran by the house, but none of the soldiers harmed the old home.

Jack and Clebe

Charlie Pointer said, "A mule was one of the primary reasons my daddy Jackson Pointer and family left the Cartwright place and moved to the Preuit Farm. My dad, Jack Pointer, agreed to buy a mule from Billy Jacobs for six dollars. At the time, Jack was making ten cents per hour. Uncle Mack McDaniel was renting Jack fifteen acres for him to farm with the mule he had purchased from Jacobs. Uncle Mack had also loaned Jack the gear and plow to make a crop; however, Jack was only able to come up with four dollars to pay on the mule, and Billy Jacobs came to take the mule."

Charlie continued, "Clebe Preuit found out that Jacobs was going to take the mule away from my dad Jack. Clebe told Jacobs not to take the mule, or he would not rent Billy Jacobs the farm field, which contained some 400 acres, if he repossessed the mule. After some negotiations, Clebe paid the remaining two dollars so that my daddy Jack could keep his mule.

"Clebe knew that my dad Jack was a hard worker and wanted his help on the Preuit Farm. Daddy agreed to move to the Preuit place but needed a house for our family. Clebe Preuit told Jack to look at the house where our family could live and use as their own, but the house was too small and had only two rooms. Therefore, Clebe got Grady Moody to help my daddy cut timber to saw into boards to make an additional room on the house. With everything worked out agreeable to all parties, our family moved to the Clebe Preuit Farm."

Clebe Preuit would give Charlie's daddy Jack and the other farmhands tickets that were good at the four stores at Wren. Jack Pointer would get in the wagon pulled by a pair of mules and go to Wren and swap the tickets for lard, meal, flour, and other food items. The ticket that Jackson carried to the store was a piece of metal about the size of a dollar bill. Wren store owners, like Will Willis, would stamp the metal ticket. Jack Pointer would sometimes buy two sides of hog meat to eat. He would also get enough corn and cotton seed to make the next crop on the Clebe Preuit Farm.

Charlie continued, "Clebe told me one day to get in his car that we were going to Moulton. Mr. Preuit bought me my first pair of shoes and two pair of overalls from Howard Delashaw's store in Moulton. Before that day, I went barefooted and wore clothes made from flour or guano (fertilizer) sacks. The day I went to the store with Mr. Clebe, I was wearing a long sack dress or shirt and did not have any shoes."

When Charlie was a small boy, he would hear Doctor Price Irwin coming down the road in his horse and buggy to see the sick folks. Charlie would run to open the gates for Doctor Price; Doctor Price would flip Charlie a nickel every time he opened a gate for him. The nickels that Doctor Price would give Charlie made a lasting memory that he cherishes to this day. Charlie thought that Doctor Price was one of the best and kindest men he had ever known. The gesture of kindness to a poor, Black country boy will never be forgotten by Charlie Pointer.

When Charlie was only eight years old, Mr. Clebe Preuit died. Charlie said, "As long as I am alive and have a good mind, I will never forget the first storebought clothes that Mr. Clebe Preuit bought for me." After Clebe's death, Charlie and his family worked for his son John Hodges Preuit.

After Jackson Pointer got too old to make the crop, Charlie continued making a crop for the Preuit family. Jackson and his sons made the crops for the Preuit Family for many years before John Preuit passed away.

Jackson and Lucy Taylor Pointer were buried in the Lindsey Memorial Garden Cemetery. The cemetery is located just one-half mile directly east of Jesse Owens Park in the Community of Oakville in Lawrence County, Alabama. From the cemetery, you can look west and see the Jesse Owens Museum and see the flags that fly in the park.

White Hodges Family

Clebe Preuit died on June 7, 1932, and his wife Sallie Hodges was born on April 9, 1875, and died on May 7, 1911. Sallie was a member of the Hodges Family of Oakville Community; her father was Doctor John Hodges. According to the 1820 Census of Lawrence County, Alabama, Fleming

Sally Hodges and John Hodges Preuit 1902

Hodges Sr. of Oakville owned 26 Black slaves. The Hodges Family were some of the wealthy slave-owning White folks of the Oakville area. Fleming Hodges' family members are buried in large stone crypts on top of the Copena Indian burial mound at the Oakville Indian Mounds Park. William Hodges, who was buried on the mound, married Sarah Walker.

William Hodges was the son of Fleming Hodges Sr. and brother to Fleming Hodges Jr. The 1850 Census of Lawrence County, Alabama, names the following: Fleming Hodges Jr. was 34 years old and born in Alabama; his wife Margaret, age 28; William, age 10; Thomas P., age seven; James F., age five; Alis, female, age three; and, Margaret, age one.

Charlie and John

Charlie Pointer, who was 89 years old at the time of our interview, said, "I also worked for Clebe Preuit and later his son John Hodges Preuit. I grew to manhood on the

Preuit Farm. For many years, I made a crop for John Preuit until he died."

Charlie continued, "If John Preuit told you something, he would do it; it was as good as money in the bank. I was at their home when both Mr. Clebe and Mr. John Preuit died. I wound up living on the Preuit Farm and making crops for John Preuit for some 50 years."

In the driest time of each year, Charlie said, "They would let me down with ropes about 50 feet into the dug well to clean it out. Every time I went into that well, I had to kill snakes that lived in there before I could start work. After we started cleaning out the well, muddy water would run out of a spring some 200 yards west of the John Preuit House. We would put something in the well, and it would come out in that spring."

Charlie said, "Each year, John Preuit would go to Florida where he owned 160 acres and bring back a truck load of apples, oranges, and pecans every Christmas. He would give us (the Jackson Pointer Family) all the fruit and pecans that we wanted. Ward Preuit, the son of John Preuit, eventually sold the farm in Florida."

Today, the old Preuit Family well that Charlie Pointer cleaned out each year is still in my back yard some 20 feet from my back porch. The spring that Charlie referred to is about 20 yards from my west property line.

Ms. Willie and Charlie

After Mr. John Preuit died, Charlie Pointer began doing farm work for Tass Jacobs. After Mr. Jacobs died,

Charlie worked for Ms. Willie Jacobs for ten years. Ms. Willie gave Charlie cash money to pay for his one acre of land where he now lives. Charlie worked for Ms. Willie Jacobs for fifty cents per day tending the cows and taking care of the farm work.

Initially, Ms. Willie told Charlie that he had to pay her a dime before she would let him work for her. Ms. Willie Jacobs told Charlie that the dime was a paid contract that he would not be late for work and would do the work that she wanted completed. Charlie said, "Ms. Willie kept that dime for many years; occasionally, she would show me the dime as a reminder of our work agreement."

Charlie would get off work on Saturday and Sunday. On Saturday morning, he would work in his garden and do the things around his house. On Saturday afternoon, Charlie would sometimes take his kids fishing to the Beaver Pond just north of Highway 36 or to the Oakville Pond. Charlie also planted and worked the garden for Ms. Willie. He had nothing but praise for his former employer, Ms. Willie Jacobs.

Charlie Pointer married Louise Price and had six children:
1. Joyce Pointer, who married Harold Freeman.
2. Charlie Pointer Jr., who married Inez Tapscott.
3. Melvin Pointer, who married Gwen Davis from Mississippi and Chicago, Illinois.
4. John Paul Pointer, who married Junita Bynum.
5. Patricia Ann Pointer (deceased), who married Doyle Wolfe.

6. Vera Dale Pointer, who married Kevin Jackson from Mt. Hope.

Oakville Baseball

When I, Rickey Butch Walker, was a small boy in the 1950s and early 1960s, most country folks like mine did not have a television, very few had radios, and many were without electricity or could not afford the cost. Therefore, community baseball was a local sport that many people enjoyed watching to pass the time, and the Black Oakville team that Charlie and his brothers played on was the very best.

The baseball teams were not allowed to play on crop land, but many cattle farming folks would allow the teams to play in their pastures. During those years, each small community including the Black folks of Oakville had a baseball team. Most of the time, the players would play ball in overalls and plow boots or barefooted.

During most baseball games, big picnics would also be a part of the festivities in order to support the team. Some folks would donate chickens and garden vegetables for the big stew pot and ice down drinks in number three wash tubs. The Black folks of the Oakville Community would have a fish fry at their baseball games. The fish would be seined from the nearby Oakville Pond. The baseball picnics were to raise money for their team to travel and to buy necessary equipment. All the items donated by the families of the Oakville players were used to raise money for the home team.

Charlie and Baseball

The greatest time in the life of Charlie Pointer was during the period that he played with his brothers and relatives for the Black Oakville baseball team. During his peak, Charlie was one of the best third basemen to ever play the game. Charlie told about people of all colors that would gather at the home field pasture of P. B. Lowery or just east of the road at the church at Oakville to watch one of the best independent Black baseball teams in the southeastern United States. Walker said, "When I was a young boy, many times I was among those spectators with my dad Brady Walker or with my Uncle Cadle Wilburn who was a pitcher on some White teams."

Charlie Pointer's greatest skill was baseball; he and older brothers Robert, Louie, Dee, and Aaron played for Oakville. When Charlie first got to play baseball with the Black team, he played in his overalls and went barefooted. After a few years of playing, Charlie and the Oakville team finally got baseball uniforms.

Charlie Pointer said, "At one time, the Oakville team had five good pitchers: Johnny Stover, Floyd Lee Stover, Lonzo Griffin, Denny Orr, and Hosey Lee Taylor. Other players on the Oakville team included Paul Pointer, John Olden Griffin, James Pig Jones, Hayward Preuit, Theo Griffin, Clifton Griffin, James Carl Brackins, Oscar Fitzgerald, Columbus Fitzgerald, Clemson Gibson, Jody Gibson, John Preuit, and Bo Jack."

The ancestors of the Black baseball players were descendants of the slaves of the local cotton plantation owners around the Oakville area. The Black Preuit baseball players got their name from the descendants of the 65 Black slaves of John William Preuit and Martha McDaniel Preuit. The Preuit Family lived about four miles west of Oakville on present-day Lawrence County Highway 211.

The Black Gibson baseball players probably got their names from the descendants of the 16 Black slaves owned by Sylvanus Gibson or the 34 Black slaves owned by Lawrence County Judge Charles Gibson. Sylvanus Gibson lived just one mile east of West Flint Creek Bridge on Highway 36, and Charles Gibson was buried in the Preuit Cemetery just two miles southwest of Speake School. At one time, Charles Gibson lived at Oakville, and he built a hog pen around the sink where the water from the Oakville Spring went underground. His hogs eventually rooted mud in the sink, closing it and creating Oakville Pond.

Charlie Pointer and his four brothers played for the Oakville baseball team which was made up entirely of Black players. Charlie said, "My older brothers Robert and Louie Pointer played ball before I was old enough, but at sixteen years of age, I got to play with my other two brothers, Aaron and Dee Pointer. Aaron would steal second base as soon as the pitcher stepped on the pad on the pitcher's mound. Me and Aaron stole every base on the field including home plate."

Mr. Charlie Pointer said, "When I started playing baseball, we would go to the games in wagons pulled by mules. One game we played Moulton and did not have the wagon; therefore, we walked from Oakville to Moulton, played the game, and walked back to Oakville. Now, all the players I started playing baseball with are dead."

At one particular game, Charlie's wife Louise was sitting watching the game when Dee Pointer fouled a fastball off his bat. The ball hit Louise so hard that it knocked her eye out. Even though she should have been knocked unconscious, Louise never dropped the baby she was holding in her arms.

Charlie played shortstop for over ten years, Aaron Pointer played second base, and his other brother Dee Pointer played first base. During the some fifteen to twenty years that he played baseball with the Oakville team, Charlie Pointer said, "I do not ever remember us losing a single game of baseball. We had two teams, when the first team got so far ahead, we would let the second team finish the game. Athens was the roughest team we played, but we still beat them. We went to Tuscaloosa and played four games in two days and won all of them. Bryant Lowery had a ton and half Chevrolet truck, and he would drive for twenty-five cents per player and would watch us play ball. When we stayed overnight, we would stay with the players of the other teams."

Charlie Pointer said, "I remembered Mr. Earl Aldridge, a long time barber in Moulton, playing for the Pinhook baseball team and Arthur Wilburn (the grandpa of Rickey Butch Walker) pitching for Pinhook. Our Oakville team played the Pinhook team in a pasture about one-quarter mile west of Elam Creek. The Pinhook baseball field at that time was west of the Preuit Farm that I grew up on and that pastureland was later bought by a Mr. King from Moulton. Later, the Pinhook team played in another pasture near the old Pinhook Church."

During my last interview with Charlie, he lived a

quiet life in his home watching television and reminiscing about the days of his youth when baseball and hard work ruled his life. While he was limited by the effects of a stroke, Charlie's eyes would light up and a big smile would come across his face when he talked about his days playing baseball. A few years ago, Mr. Charlie Pointer passed away, as all the other Black baseball legends of Oakville.

Babe Ruth Taylor

The Babe Ruth of Oakville was given the birth name of James Andrew Taylor, but that baseball legend was known by locals as Buddy Taylor or Babe Ruth Taylor. Buddy lived along with many of his family members in the Community of Oakville. The mixed Black and White community was not far from my childhood home at Speake and my present-day home of the original Preuit Farm.

Charlie Pointer said, "I was a first cousin to Babe Ruth Taylor. He was the main player, leader, and coach of our Oakville baseball team. Buddy Taylor and many of the other players from the Oakville team were farm laborers for John Wiley, John McCay, Tass Jacobs, Clebe Preuit, and Bryant Lowery."

The Black Oakville baseball team played many of their baseball games in P. B. (Bryant) Lowery's cow pasture on the west side of the Oakville Road. They also played on the east side of the road just north of the present-day Jesse Owens Park near where a church now stands.

I, Rickey Butch Walker, remember Mr. Jimmy Speake, who was an attorney in Moulton for years, telling me that some of the best Black baseball players that he had ever seen and coached against were from Oakville. One player in particular that Speake liked was called Babe Ruth Taylor. Jimmy Speake said, "Babe Ruth Taylor could knock a baseball over 500 feet on a regular basis, and he should have been a major league baseball player. The Black Babe Ruth from Oakville was one of the best baseball players to ever play the game."

Charlie said, "A baseball scout came down from the New York Yankees, and he watched our team play four or five games. The scout stayed for two weeks trying to get Buddy 'Babe Ruth' Taylor, me, and my brothers Aaron and Dee Pointer to try out for the New York Yankees, but we were not about to move to New York City. He tried to get us to go north to play professional baseball, but we all refused to go."

Buddy's son Rayford Taylor said, "My daddy went up north one time to try out for professional baseball but did not want to stay away from his family or leave his Oakville home." Buddy just did not fit in with the big city life and atmosphere, and he chose to return home to play baseball with his relatives and friends.

Charlie Pointer, who was a teammate of Buddy Taylor, said, "Babe Ruth Taylor was definitely one of the best baseball players to ever play the game for Oakville. I do not remember us ever losing a game."

My Uncle Cadle Wilburn was a member of some of the cow pasture baseball teams; he played and pitched for Speake, Wren, and Pinhook. He spent most of his amateur baseball playing with the Pinhook team that, for a long time, had their home field in the pasture of Mr. Ben McMillan of the Pinhook Community. He said, "One of the best baseball teams that I ever played against was the Black team from Oakville; Babe Ruth (Buddy Taylor) would knock a homerun nearly every time the ball went over home plate."

Charlie said, "In his early days, Babe Ruth Taylor was both a left- and right-handed pitcher, but after one of his fast pitches caused a fatality, Babe Ruth chose to play catcher. He had the ability to play any position on the baseball field. Taylor doubled for many years as a player/ coach for the team. He could throw a runner out at second base without even standing up."

His son Rayford Taylor told me, "If a man was on first base, dad would say to the pitcher, 'Let him run, I got him.' Seldom did a runner ever steal second base when my daddy was catcher."

At the time that Buddy Taylor was catching baseballs, it was legal for the catcher to chatter, and he was constantly chattering to the batter. Buddy would say, "You can't hit what you can't see, and the bat must have a hole in it." As a young boy, I loved to hear Buddy Taylor chatter at a baseball game.

Also, Buddy Taylor had a feel for the baseball; he would tell the players "this ball is dead, and we are not going to play with it anymore." From all that people have said about Babe Ruth Taylor, you could tell that he had a deep passion and love for the game of baseball.

James Andrew "Babe Ruth" Taylor also had a son that was a great baseball pitcher; his name was Hosey Lee Taylor. Before my dad Brady Walker died, he and I would

143

stop by the home of Mr. Hosey Lee and give him and his wife a bunch of fish that we had caught. They were always very appreciative of our gesture.

Besides Hosey Lee Taylor, Babe Ruth Taylor had other sons that played baseball: Wyman Taylor, Wayne Taylor, and Rayford Taylor. Hosey would usually start the game pitching left-handed, and about halfway through the game he would switch to pitching right-handed.

Mr. Rayford Taylor, the son of Babe Ruth Taylor, told me, "The Oakville team finally raised enough money to buy uniforms and equipment. The team would get together and seine Oakville Pond. The fish we caught would be cooked and sold at the baseball game to make enough money for the team's expenses. We would fry the fish, and then sell fish sandwiches and cold drinks to the spectators that came to watch the home games."

Walker said, "I was very fortunate to be one of those spectators when my Uncle Cadle Wilburn pitched for the Pinhook Team. Pinhook was never able to beat the all-Black Oakville baseball team with Babe Ruth Taylor behind home plate."

Walker continued, "Years after his death, everyone north of the Black Warrior Mountains in the Oakville area of Lawrence County had heard of the baseball exploits of Buddy 'Babe Ruth' Taylor. It was an honor for me as a young boy to watch the legendary Babe Ruth Taylor play baseball at Oakville. To this day, I remember the crack of that bat when Babe Ruth Taylor would hit a homerun."

Babe and Emma

Babe Ruth Taylor, the grandson of a former slave, and Emma Williams Taylor had 17 children. Buddy encouraged his kids and grandkids to play ball because he loved the game with all his being.

**Emma Louise Williams and James
Andrew (Babe Ruth) Taylor**

After he got too old to play baseball, Babe Ruth Taylor coached a girls' softball team that was also very good. Many of the children and grandchildren of Babe Ruth and Emma Taylor still live near the Oakville Community.

Cannon House

The picture of James Andrew "Babe Ruth" Taylor and his wife Emma Louise Williams was taken in front of the old Jim Cannon house just west of the West Fork of Flint Creek. The Taylor family lived on the place where Jesse Owens' folks had worked prior to moving north for better opportunities.

For many years, Babe Ruth and his family owned and lived in the old J. C. Cannon House, which was built in

1890. The house was on a knoll about hundred yards west of the West Fork of Flint Creek in the Community of Oakville in Lawrence County, Alabama. After Babe Ruth Taylor, the old house was owned by the late Mr. Don Alexander, who worked to save the historic home.

The Cannon House is just north of Highway 157 and just west of the bridge crossing the West Fork of Flint Creek. Heading east toward Cullman and just prior to crossing the bridge on Highway 157, you can see the Cannon House across the farm fields to the north.

Jim Cannon and his wife Minnie McLemore eventually moved to Moulton, Alabama. Jim was elected Sheriff of Lawrence County. Today, the Jim Cannon house is still standing.

Jim Cannon House

Jesse Owens

Another famous Black Lawrence County family that had ties to the J. C. Cannon place near Oakville was Henry Cleveland Owens and Mary Emma Fitzgerald. They were the parents of the Olympic great James Cleveland (Jesse)

Owens. Henry, the father of Jesse, lived in a sharecroppers shack about 100 yards north of the Cannon House. Henry worked for Mr. Cannon prior to moving to Cleveland, Ohio.

According to the 1847 tax list of Lawrence County, Alabama, Isaac N. Owen, a White cotton planter, owned a Black slave known as Henry, who was the grandfather of Jesse Owens. Henry had a son who was named Henry Cleveland Owens. The Black family of Owens took their last name from the Owen Estate in Lawrence County. After the Civil War, several of the slaves of Isaac N. Owen added an "s" to their last name and became Owens.

The Owen Plantation was the namesake of Owen Chapel Church in the present-day Community of Youngtown, some five to seven miles east of Mt. Hope School and some three to four miles south of Landersville Community in Lawrence County, Alabama. The church and community lie along the north edge of the Black Warrior Mountains, within one mile north of the Indian trail known as High Town Path (present-day Ridge Road) which follows the Tennessee Divide through Lawrence County.

Youngtown got its name from Reason Young, who according to the 1860 Census of Lawrence County slave schedules owned 20 Black slaves. The Young family owned a vast estate in the area that extended from the edge of the mountain to Landersville. In addition, Youngtown became one of the largest reconstruction schools for Black children in the area after the Civil War.

As I was interviewing folks in the area for my book *Warrior Mountains Folklore*, I heard many stories about long lines of Black children walking the dusty country roads every morning and afternoon heading to and from the

Black school at Youngtown. Today, the Black school has long since been torn down, and very few if any Black folks remain in the area of Youngtown. I remember the old two-story wooden Black school that sat about one mile west of present-day Owen Chapel Church. The school was located in the 90-degree curve just west of the church.

After Henry Cleveland Owens and Mary Emma Fitzgerald married, they moved to the J. C. Cannon place just west of the Community of Oakville. They lived in a small wooden house that was located just south and behind the Jim Cannon house. Henry worked for Mr. Cannon, but as it was with most Black families, they could never get ahead; they worked at grueling farm labor just to keep their family from starving.

Since the West Fork of Flint Creek was the line between the Oakville and Pinhook Precincts, it appears that the family of Henry Cleveland Owens was living on the J. C. Cannon place at the time James Cleveland "Jesse" Owens was born on September 12, 1913. During the time of Jesse's birth, the Henry Owens family was listed in the Pinhook Precinct.

When Jesse Owens was about nine years old, the Henry Owens family moved north to Cleveland, Ohio. While a student in the Cleveland schools, a teacher asked for his name, to which he replied J. C. Owens. Whether it was a misunderstanding or not, from that time forward, the teacher called him Jesse which stuck.

During the 1936 Olympic Games in Berlin, Germany, Jesse Owens won four gold medals. His remarkable wins embarrassed the White supremacy ruler Adolph Hitler.

State Representative Roger Dutton, who was a friend of mine, pursued the placement of a monument to Jesse Owens on the Lawrence County Courthouse Square when he was serving in the State of Alabama House of Representatives. His intention was to honor the Black Olympic hero who

Jesse Owens
1936 Olympics

was born in our county, but the White political structure of Lawrence County effectively blocked the placement of the monument for Jesse Owens on the courthouse square.

I remember Roger telling me that he wanted to see the ivory towers of Lawrence County's political structure crumble and fall. Therefore, not to be outdone, Roger got funds provided to buy a small rectangular block of property at the road junction in the Community of Oakville for placement of the Jesse Owens Monument. Originally, the monument was just west and across the road from the present-day Jesse Owens Park. Roger Dutton died before seeing his dream come to fruition. He was buried in the Naylor Family Cemetery at Bulah Church near my great-great-great-grandmother, Mary Elizabeth Welborn Segars Naylor.

Marvin Fitzgerald, a dear departed Black friend, along with other Black and White leaders, worked tirelessly to ensure that his cousin Jesse Owens was appropriately honored. After several years, additional land was purchased on the east side of the road for the Jesse Owens Park. The park was strongly supported by then Lawrence County Commissioner Larry LouAllen. During his tenure, LouAllen worked with the Lawrence County Commission to ensure the Jesse Owens Park and the adjacent Oakville Indian Mounds Park, which I was over, received their fair share of funding.

Today, Jesse Owens Park at Oakville in Lawrence County, Alabama, has worldwide recognition. The museum in the park tells the story of one of the most famous Black athletes—James Cleveland (Jesse) Owens, the grandson of a former slave of Isaac N. Owen.

Bessie Smith

Laura was a Black slave baby listed on the 1847 tax list of Lawrence County, Alabama; she belonged to Isaac Nabors Owen, a White cotton plantation owner. In the 1860 Lawrence County, Alabama, Census, Isaac N. Owen owned 29 Black slaves. The Owen cotton plantation was west of Moulton, Alabama. Two of the Owen slaves were the ancestors of two very famous Black legends—Jesse Owens and Bessie Smith.

In 1847, Laura was a very young child/baby; she was born into slavery. Laura, the former slave of Isaac N. Owen, became the mother of the famous Blues legend known as Bessie Smith.

Bessie Smith

Shortly after the Civil War, William Smith and Laura Owens were married; they became the parents of Bessie Smith. William became a Black Baptist parson or preacher in Moulton, Alabama.

According to the 1870 Census of Lawrence County, Alabama, William Smith was listed as a Black minister of the gospel in Moulton, Alabama. William preached in the Smith Chapel Tabernacle in Moulton which was located on the land given to the church by the White cotton planter Isaac Nabors Owen and his wife.

It appears for some reason that William and Laura Owens Smith moved from Moulton, Alabama, to Chattanooga, Tennessee. Bessie Smith was born on April 15, 1894, in Chattanooga, Tennessee. By the time Bessie was nine years old, her parents were dead. Viola Smith was the older sister of Bessie, and she took charge of raising her siblings; therefore, Bessie Smith lived with her sister until she was old enough to be on her own.

From former Lawrence County slaves, Bessie Smith eventually became known as "The Empress of the Blues." During her time, Bessie became the highest paid Black singer and entertainer in the United States. She had many recordings with Columbia Records; Bessie Smith was considered the "First Lady of Blues Music."

In 1929, Bessie Smith was in a movie based on W. C. Handy's song known as the "St. Louis Blues." Handy, who was the Father of the Blues, was born in Florence, Alabama, where he is honored each year for his contributions to Blues music.

Bessie Smith died as a result of terrible car crash on September 26, 1937; she was on United States Route 61 between Memphis, Tennessee, and Clarksdale, Mississippi. The delay of the arrival of the ambulance contributed to her death.

Some say if Bessie had been carried to the White hospital in Clarksville that she would have survived the car accident; however, the time it took to get her to the G. T. Thomas Afro-American Hospital did not help her chances of survival, and she died in the hospital.

Bessie Smith was buried in Philadelphia at the Mount Lawn Cemetery. Finally, on August 7, 1970, singer Janis Joplin provided money and support to erect a tombstone for Bessie Smith.

Huston Cobb Jr. Interviews

During the 1980s, Mr. Huston Cobb Jr. interviewed several elderly Black Folks in the area of the Muscle Shoals of northwest Alabama. A frequently asked question by Mr. Cobb was, "Where did you go to school?" In 1934, there were 19 schools for Black children in Colbert County, Alabama.

Most of the schools for Black children were very small and scattered across the county because most children had to walk to school. The schools for the Black community were as follows: Barton, Bethel, Bishop, Cave Springs, Cherokee, Hawkins Creek, Lane Springs, Leighton Training, Liberty, Margerum, Mt. Olivia (Pond Creek), Mt. Pleasant, New Home, Pride, Ricks (The Oaks), Riverton, Spring Valley, St. James, and St. Paul.

Much of the interview information of Huston Cobb Jr. was verified with census records; however, Black families were not enumerated in the census records prior to the Civil War. From 1870 in each 10-year period, census records differ on race identification, age, year of birth, and the spelling of both the first and last names. Even though the handwritten records contain many mistakes, the censuses are the most reliable historical documents we have on early Black and White families of the Muscle Shoals area.

The following are portions of the interviews that Mr. Huston Cobb Jr. conducted and that he provided for this book. The Black folks that Mr. Cobb interviewed have passed away, and he probably got their last stories. The Black folks written about below were listed in alphabetical order by last name.

Bailey, Hirmon "Haney"

About 1981, Huston Cobb Jr. interviewed Hirmon "Haney" Bailey, who was 92 years old at the time of the interview. The parents of Haney were Bolin Bailey and Ann M. Dickson Bailey.

The Black family name of Bailey probably came from White cotton planters and slave owners with that last name. There are not any known records of Black folks in northwest Alabama owning Black slaves. According to the 1850 Franklin (Colbert) County, Alabaman Census, C. C. Bailey, a White man, owned 31 Black slaves. In the 1860 Franklin (Colbert) County census, Joseph J. Bailey, a White man, owned 36 Black slaves.

Bolin Bailey

On April 19, 1876, Bolin Bailey married Ann M. Dickson in Colbert County, Alabama. They were married by Bolin King M.G.; however, Bolin marked the marriage license with an "X" because he could not write.

According to the 1880 Colbert County, Alabama, Census, Bolin Bailey was a 24-year-old Black male farmer. Other family members in his household were as follows: Ann Maria Bailey, Wife, 23; Martin Bailey, Son, four; Mary Bailey, Daughter, two; and Susanna Bailey, Daughter, one. Bolin Bailey and his wife Ann M. Dickson were born into slavery.

In the 1900 Colbert County, Alabama, Census, Precinct 16, Sheffield, Household 72, Bolin Bailey was a 46-year-old Black male born in January 1854 in Alabama and married for 23 years. Also in his household were the following: Annie M. Bailey, Wife, Female, 40, born February 1860, Alabama, married 23 years, 9 births, 8 now living; Daisy Bailey, Daughter, Female, 18, born October 1882, Alabama; Robert Bailey, Son, Male, 16, born May 1884, Alabama; Lena Bailey, Daughter, Female, 12, born March 1888, Alabama; Hirmon (Haney) Bailey, Son, Male, 11, born September 1889, Alabama; and John Bailey, Son, Male, 10, born June 1890.

Haney Bailey

Based on the 1900 census, Hirmon "Haney" Bailey was born in 1889. In the census, Bolin was listed as a farmer, and his two sons Robert and Haney were listed as farm laborers. At 11 years old, Haney was working with his father and brother on the farm.

While Haney Bailey lived at Pond Creek, he married Mattie Mullins. She was the daughter of Daylough "Dalue" Mullins and Ella King Mullins. On December 28, 1893, Dalue Mullins married Ella King in Lawrence County, Alabama.

Sallie Mullins

The parents of Dalue Mullins were never married. His father was George Granville Spangler, who was born a slave in 1846. The mother of Dalue was Sallie Mullins, who was born a slave in 1851.

The Mulatto children of Sallie Mullins and George Granville Spangler were as follows: Molly Mullins (1867–1948); Edward Mullins (1870–?); Daylou (Dalue) Mullins

(1871–?); Love Mullins (1874–?); Perley Mullins (1874–?); John Mullins (1879–1954); Willie Mullins (1880–?); Mattie Mullins (1883–1936); and Jake Mullins (1887–?).

The 1880 Lawrence County, Alabama, Census, Beat 4, Leighton, Township 5 had the following information: Sallie Mullins, Female, Black, 29, Head of Household, Alabama; Mollie Mullins, Daughter, Female, 12, Alabama; Edward Mullins, Son, Male, 10, Alabama; Dalue Mullins, Son, Male, eight, Alabama; Perley Mullins, Daughter, Female, six, Alabama; Love Mullins, Daughter, Female, six, Alabama; Matt Mullins (She became the wife of Haney Bailey.), Daughter, Female, four, Alabama; Willie Mullins, Son, Male, 0, Alabama.

Dalue and Ella

According to the 1910 Colbert County, Alabama, Census, Leighton, Daylaugh (Dalue) Mullins was a 38-year-old Mulatto male who was married. Also in his household were the following: Ella Mullins, Wife, Female, 32, Alabama; Annie L. Mullins, Daughter, Female, nine, Alabama; Mattie L. Mullins (She became the wife of Haney Bailey.), Daughter, Female, seven, Alabama; Otis Mullins, Son, Male, five, Alabama; Daylaugh Mullins, Son, Male, three, Alabama; Walter F. Mullins, Son, Male, 0, Alabama.

In the 1920 Colbert County, Alabama, Census, Leighton, Daylaugh (Dalue) Mullen was a 48-year-old Mulatto male. In his household were the following: Ella Mullen, Wife, Female, 44, Alabama; Mattie Mullen (She became the wife of Haney Bailey.), Daughter, Female, 17, Alabama; Otis Mullen, Son, Male, 17, Alabama; Daylaugh Mullen Jr., Son, Male, 12, Alabama; Walter F. Mullen, Son, Male, 10, Alabama.

In the 1930 Colbert County, Alabama, Census, Leighton, Doylue (Dalue) Mullen was a 59-year-old Mulatto male who was married. In his household were the following: Ella Mullen, Wife; Doylue Mullen Jr., Son; Walter F. Mullen, Son; and James E. Mullen.

In the 1940 Colbert County, Alabama, Census, Precinct 11, Leighton, Dalue Mullens was a 67-year-old Mulatto male who was married. In his household were the following: Ella Mullen, Wife; and Walter F. Mullen, Son. Dalue and Ella only had a third-grade education.

According to the 1940 Colbert County, Alabama, Census, Sheffield, Elvin Mullens, a brother of Mattie Mullens Bailey, was 39 years old and married to Katie Mullens, who was 37. Their children were: Walter Frank Mullens, son, 17; Margaret Mullens, Daughter, 14; Willie B. Mullens, Daughter, 12; and Perch Jerry Mullens, Son, nine.

Daylue Mullins Jr. died in 1972 in Colbert County. Walter F. Mullins died 1974 in Colbert County. In addition, Walter Frank Mullens, son of Elvin and Katie, was born about 1923, and he died on June 26, 2004. The young Walter F. Mullins was buried in Colbert Memorial Gardens at Tuscumbia, Alabama.

World War I

Haney Bailey fought in World War I. Other Black fellow World War I soldiers who left with Haney Bailey from Colbert County included Arthur Jarmon, Charlie McDuffy, Limon Bates, Alfred Smith, and Arthur Johnson.

Haney Bailey was on a ship for 18 days before reaching France. He served 18 months during the war, with the majority of his time being in France. He came home in 1919, and he first landed in New York. He was mustered out in Georgia.

Haney and Mattie

Initially after arriving home from his military service, Haney started farming. Not long after beginning to farm, Haney married Mattie Mullins.

Based on the census records, Haney Bailey and Mattie Mullins were probably married between 1920 and 1930. In 1920, Mattie was living with her parents, and she was listed as 17 years old. She was not listed with her mother and father in 1930.

When Haney Bailey was farming, he took his cotton to be ginned at Underwood Crossroads. He transported his cotton by wagon from Pond Creek to the Gin. Haney said, "I left farming in 1926, and my wife and I moved to Leighton. I can remember when they had a saloon in Leighton."

Later, Haney Bailey went to work at TVA at Wilson Dam. Haney worked up and down the river from Wheeler Dam, Guntersville Dam, Douglas Dam, and Fort Loudon Dam at Lenoir City, Tennessee.

After a severe accident while at work with TVA, Haney had a broken back, collar bone, and three broken ribs. A huge boulder rock fell on him and crushed several bones. After getting out of the hospital, he was sent to Memphis for three weeks and then to Muscle Shoals, where he retired in 1958.

Haney and Mattie lived in Leighton until they died. Records of their death and burial were not located.

Bates, Rosella Savage Roland

On October 24, 1981, Huston Cobb Jr. interviewed Rosella (Rozelle) Savage Roland Bates. In 1981, Rosella Savage Bates was the only one of the Savage siblings that was still alive. Rosella was living in Cleveland, Ohio, at that time. Sally Mae Fuqua Thomas, who was a half-sister to Rosella, was also living in 1981.

Rosella was born on March 8, 1898, in Lawrence County, Alabama. Rosella was the daughter of Tom Savage and Callie Cobb Savage. Callie was born in 1868, and she was the daughter of Archie and Candice Cobb.

Tom Savage and Callie Cobb Savage had 10 children, which included six boys and four girls. The children of Tom and Callie Savage were: (1) Mattie Savage Fuqua, (2) Leon Savage, (3) Coleman "Coaley" Savage, (4) Zafari Savage, (5) Naomi Savage, (6) Gertrude Savage, (7) Rosella Savage, (8) Tommy Savage, who married Fannie Lou Savage, (9) Lovell Savage, and (10) Elton Savage.

Archie and Candice Cobb

Rosella Savage was only five years old when her father, Tom Savage, passed in 1903. At the time of his death, the family was living at a place called Knob Hill. After her husband Tom Savage passed away, Callie Cobb Savage moved the family to the home of her father and mother, Archie and Candice Cobb.

159

According to the 1880 Federal Census of South Florence in Colbert County, Alabama, Archie Cobb was 48 years old and his wife Candas (Candice) Cobb was 47 years old. In 1880, Archie and Candas Cobb had the following children living in their household: Henry Cobb, Son, Male, 18; Malinda Cobb, Daughter, Female, 15; Caroline "Callie" Cobb, Daughter, Female, 12; Frank Cobb, Son, Male, eight; Mary Frances Cobb, Daughter, Female, six; Sally Cobb, Daughter, Female, four; and Ada Cobb, Daughter, Female, one.

Candice Cobb, the mother of Callie, was a sister to Anna Liza Cobb. The daughter of Anna was Ella Cobb, who was a first cousin of Callie Cobb. Ella married Mathias Carter; they had two children, Zoey and Theodor.

Tom Cobb, an older brother of Callie, was the son of Archie and Candas, and Tom had already moved out by 1880. Originally, Tom Cobb and his wife, Cindy Foster, lived south of Bethel Church in Colbert County. They later moved to an area known as Pond Creek. Tom died while living at Pond Creek. Melvin Cobb was one of the sons of Tom Cobb.

After living with Archie and Candice Cobb, Callie Cobb Savage moved her family to the Morris Farm to make a crop; there, the family did farm labor. While living there, the home that the family of Callie lived in caught fire and burned.

Rosella said, "I liked to got burned, but mother got me, and I went out. When I went outdoors, I got to thinking about my new shoes bought in the spring of the year. After thinking about my slippers, I went back in the burning house in mother's front room, and I got my shoes and came back out."

William Henry Fuqua

Shortly after losing their home, Callie Cobb Savage married a second time to William Henry Fuqua. According to Rosella, "William was a very nice man and great stepfather."

William Henry Fuqua and Callie Cobb Savage Fuqua had one daughter, Sally Mae Fuqua. Sally Mae married Jed T. Thomas, and they moved to Chattanooga, Tennessee.

In the 1910 Colbert County, Alabama, Census, Brickville, Household 28, Family 29, William H. Fuqua was listed as the head of his household. William was a 46-year-old Mulatto male farmer born in Alabama. Also in the household were the following: Callie (Callie Cobb Savage Fuqua), wife, Black, female, 42, March 4, 11 children, Alabama; Sallie May Fuqua, daughter, Black, female, three, Alabama; Mattie Savage, stepdaughter, Black female, 25, single, farm laborer, Alabama; Lion (Leon) Savage, stepson, Black, male, 21, single, farm laborer, Alabama; Coleman "Coaley" Savage, stepson, Black, male, 20, single, farm laborer, Alabama; Gophora, stepson, Black male, 19, single, farm laborer, Alabama; Gertrude Savage, stepdaughter, Black, female, 16, farm laborer, at school, Alabama; Rozelle Savage, stepdaughter, Black, female, 13, farm laborer, at school, Alabama; Tomie Savage, stepson, Black, male, 11, farm laborer, at school, Alabama; Lovell Savage, stepson, Black, male, 10, farm laborer, at school, Alabama; Elton Savage, stepson, Black, male, eight, at school, Alabama; Houston Cobb (father of Huston Cobb Jr.), grandson, Black, male, seven, at school, Alabama; Melinda Dixon, aunt, Black female, 72, widow, 1 child, Alabama; plus 1 servant.

In 1910, Houston Cobb, father of Huston Cobb Jr., was living in the household of his step-grandfather William Henry Fuqua. At the time, he was living in an extended family; Houston was only seven years old.

Rosella Savage Roland

Rosella Savage married Delmer Roland, and they had three children: Willa Berta Roland, Clarence James (Jim) Roland, and J. B. Roland.

According to the 1920 Lawrence County, Alabama, Census, Courtland, Household 158, Family 144, enumerated 15 January 1920, was the following: Fuqua, William, head, Black, male, 51, mar, farmer, Alabama; Callie, wife, Black, female, 52, mar, Alabama; Sallie Mae, daughter, (actual age was 13), widowed, at school, Alabama; Tom Savage, stepson, Black, male, 18 (actual age was 21), single, at school, Alabama; Lovell Savage, stepson, Black, male, 14 (actual age was 20), at school, Alabama; Elton Savage, son, Black, male, 12 (actual age was 18), at school, Alabama; Rosella Savage, stepdaughter, Black, female, 11 (actual age was 23), at school, Alabama; Estelle, daughter, Black, female, 10, at school, Alabama; Alabama; William, son, Black, male, seven, at school, Alabama; Willmar, daughter, Black, female, six, Alabama; Jim, grandson (step-grandson), Black, male, three, Alabama; J.B., grandson (step-grandson), Black, male, one, Alabama.

In the 1920 census, Tom, Lovell, Elton, and Rosella were the children Tom Savage and Callie Cobb; they were stepchildren of William Henry Fuqua. The grandsons, Jim Roland and J. B. Roland, were the step-grandsons of William Henry Fuqua; they were the sons of Delmer and Rosella Savage Roland.

The 1930 Lawrence County, Alabama, Census, Town Creek, Household 58, Family 58, enumerated April 12, 1930, listed the following: William Fuqua, head, Black, male, 17, farmer, Alabama; William H., grandfather, Black, male, 60, mar 20, farm laborer, Alabama; Callie, grandmother, Black, female, 65, mar 25, farm laborer, Alabama.

In the 1930 census, William Cullen Fuqua was listed as the head of the household and as the 17-year-old grandson of William Henry Fuqua. In the 1920 census, the young William was listed as a seven-year-old son, but he was actually a grandson.

According to Rosella, "Callie helped her husband William raise his grandson, William Cullen Fuqua. William (Cullen) got shot in the head and killed by Ed Geralds. After being shot, William lived for less than one week."

Willa Berta Roland, daughter of Rosella, married Marshall Donna. They had one daughter, Clentelle Donna Campbell, who had five children. Willa died on May 4, 1979, while she was living in Cleveland, Ohio.

Clarence James (Jim) Roland went hunting with his younger brother J. B. Roland in the fall of the year. During their hunting trip, Jim got shot accidently in one of his legs, which the doctor had to amputate.

Rosella, the mother of Jim, said, "Jim got well from the loss of his leg, and he went everywhere he wanted to go, including places to my people to spend the night. He was a beautiful boy who was so nice and so industrious that he just did not allow anyone to go to the farm unless he would go out there with them. He could not stand to see part of the family working unless he was trying to be right with them, which he could not do it because he did not have his other leg. He would go, get tired, and sit on the damp ground while taking his break every morning. He got along just fine for about two years or better, but later on, he got the eight-day pneumonia and passed away."

Rosella Savage Roland Bates

Rosella Savage Roland later married Raymond T. "Uncle Tobbie" D. Bates. They lived at Wooten Field before moving near Lake Jackson on Sixth Street in Colbert County, Alabama.

After living a year on Sixth Street, Uncle Tobbie and Rosella moved from Colbert County to Town Creek in Lawrence County. After living at Town Creek for two years, Uncle Tobbie passed away, and Rosella moved to Chattanooga, Tennessee.

Rosella said, "I just picked up and went on to Chattanooga, Tennessee, so I could put my grandbaby Clentelle in school. I went up there and got a sewing job. My grandbaby finished school in Chattanooga; Clentelle married a Campbell."

In 1940, while Rosella was living in Chattanooga, her stepfather, William Henry Fuqua, died. Rosella said,

"He got sick and passed, and my mother lived two more years after his death." When Callie Cobb Savage Fuqua died in the 1940s, the family was living near Childers's Store in Lawrence County.

Rosella Visits Houston

After living in Chattanooga, Rosella moved to Cleveland, Ohio. Rosella said, "I came to Alabama to visit with my Brother Tommy Savage's two sons. They live in Buffalo, New York. They came through Cleveland and picked me up, and brought me down here, and I was so glad to get to come. And I had called Houston, and he lives alone now. I had called him and I said, 'Houston, I'm coming down there. Can I stay with you? I want to stay right there with you at your home.' He said, 'Yes girl! Come on, I'd be glad to have you!' So I came with Thomas and Green. They came to see their mother. She was sick."

Houston Cobb asked, "You plan to go back when?" Rosella replied, "Well, I guess the boys, they say they have seen everybody and had such a good time. So I don't want them to overdo it, so I guess we will be leaving maybe tomorrow. Maybe we'll leave Sunday."

Huston Cobb Jr. inquired, "And you don't know when you plan to come back?" To which Rosella replied, "Oh no, but I wish I could stay a little while longer, but I'm not gonna hold the boys up since they've been so nice to bring me. I haven't seen all of these kids of Houston's yet. I want to see all of them cause every one of them's sweet, and they're so nice to me. But, I just can't see them all because I'll be leaving I guess tomorrow. Well, I'll see them next time."

Mattie Cobb

Rosella said, "Yeah, Mattie had one son, and the son was named Houston. We all would tease her about Houston. Uh, she didn't have many children, but she had that one son Houston, and he brought her lots of children. He brought her seven children."

Rosella continued "Houston was a beautiful boy. He was just one of the most industrious guys you ever seen. He was kinda small you know, and he was just sweet. We all just loved him. I help her take care of him when he was a small kid. I'm just so crazy about Houston. I always loved him. He had the sweetest kids. He had two girls and five sons, so he had seven kids.

"I told Mattie... I said, 'Mattie, that makes up for you since you didn't have but one. Now your son came along, and now you've got seven.' She said, 'Yes, I'm so proud of my seven grandkids, I don't know what to do. And they are beautiful children, all of them. They are just so smart, all of them.'"

Rosella recalled, "I can't remember one that did not graduate. Some went to college. They're just nice. I've never seen no kids like 'em. They're just sweet as they can be! And they all is married. Every one of them is married. Got them beautiful homes. I just don't know what to say about a family like that. I hope that they just continue to be nice."

Death of Rosella Bates

On December 1, 1990, Ms. Rosella Savage Roland

Bates died in Sheffield in Colbert County, Alabama. Rosella was buried in the Bethel Colbert Missionary Baptist Church Cemetery in Colbert County.

Brawley, Ida Little

In 1985, Huston Cobb Jr. did a short interview with Mrs. Ida Little Brawley, who was 81 years old. At the time of the interview, Ida had seven grandchildren and one great-grandchild.

The Black family names of Little and Brawley probably came from White slave owners in the area. According to the 1850 Franklin (Colbert) County, Alabama, Census, Edward Little was a White owner of 26 Black slaves. Also in the 1850 Lauderdale County, Alabama, Census, a White woman by the name of Sarah Brawly owned five Black slaves.

Mt. Pleasant

Ida was born on January 15, 1904, at Mt. Pleasant, north of Leighton, Alabama. She basically lived her entire life in the Mt. Pleasant Community on the County Line Road in Colbert County, Alabama.

At the time of the interview, Ida was still living in the old home place of her family near Mt. Pleasant. She and her husband had a house built which burned down. They rebuilt, and she was living in that home when she was interviewed.

Ida went to a little one-room school at Mt. Pleasant across the road from the graveyard on the west side of the

County Line Road. Mattie Johnson was a teacher from Courtland that taught her. Ida later attended a three-room Rosenwald school that was built for Black students at Mt. Pleasant.

Walter and Anna

The parents of Ida Little Brawley were Walter Little Sr. and Anna L. Madden. The Black family name of Madden probably came from Elisha Madding, a White cotton planter in Lawrence County who owned 62 Black slaves in 1850.

The 1920 Colbert County, Alabama, Census, Leighton Precinct, Household Identification Number 71, on January 8, 1920, by enumerator N. R. Young listed the following information: Walter Little, head of his household, was a 38-year-old Mulatto born about 1882 in Alabama. His mother and father were also born in Alabama.

The 1920 census included the following: Anner Little, wife of Walter, was 35 years old born about 1885 in Alabama. The following children were listed as Mulatto as follows: Sallie Mae Little, daughter, female, 18; Clearo Little, daughter, female, 17; Ida Little, daughter, female, 15; Carrie Little, daughter, female, 13; Walter Little Jr., son, male, 10; Ginea (Geneva), daughter, female, eight; Mattie Little, daughter, female, six; Sadiedel " Sadie" Little, daughter, female, five; Rerce-el Little, son, male, three; and Frank Lucil Little, daughter, female, eight mo.

Additional information in the 1920 census indicates that the father, Walter Little, could not read or write. The mother, Anner, and all children seven years old or older could read or write. They were renting their house at the time of the census.

The 1920 census did not include the older sister of Ida. Her oldest sister was Fannie Mae Little Adams, who had already married and moved out of the household at the time of the census.

Sallie Mae Little, another sister of Ida, was married to Timothy Vinson on April 11, 1920, at Mt. Pleasant Church by N. Tompkins, Judge of Probate. Sallie Mae Little Vinson died in Sheffield in 1951 at 49 years of age.

The Black family name of Vinson probably came from the White cotton planter by the name of Drury Vinson. He owned 107 Black slaves in 1850 near Leighton in Colbert County.

Huston and Ida

According to the marriage license document of April 5, 1924, the following information was on file in Colbert County, Alabama. Huston Brawley was 22 years old, and Ida Little was 19 years old at the time the marriage license was issued. Huston was six feet two inches tall, and Ida was five feet eight inches tall. Huston weighed 169 pounds, and Ida weighed 135 pounds. This was the first marriage for both, and they were born in Alabama. There was no blood relationship betwixt the two parties, and both were Protestants. Huston was listed as a farm laborer, and their address was given as Leighton, Alabama.

The marriage between Huston Brawley and Ida Little actually took place on April 6, 1924. They were married at Mt. Pleasant Church on the County Line Road by Reverend I. B. Abernathy. After their marriage, the couple lived at the old home place of Ida in the Mt. Pleasant Community north of Leighton in Colbert County.

Family of Huston Brawley

Huston Brawley was born about 1903; his parents were Frank Brawley and Virgena "Jennie" Abernathy. Frank Brawley was born about 1862; he was listed a Baptist clergyman. Jennie was born about 1866. Both of Huston's parents were born in Alabama.

The siblings of Huston were the following: Samantha, sister, born about 1888; Eldridge, brother, born about 1889; Marie, sister, born about 1892; Laura, sister, born about 1893; Blanche, sister, born about 1895; Willie, brother, born about 1897; Flem, brother, born about 1899; Longertha, sister, born about 1904; and Edward, brother, born about 1906.

In the 1940 Colbert County, Alabama, Census, Huston and Ida are listed with one son, whose name was Jones Brawley or James Brawley. At the time of the census, their son Jones or James was 13 years old.

Death of Huston and Ida

Huston Brawley, husband of Ida, died on March 13, 1956. Ida remembered some of her husband's siblings, which included Lee Brawley, who married Anna Bell Johnson, James Brawley, and Jackson Brawley who were his older brothers.

On May 29, 1995, Ida Brawley died at the age of 91 in Colbert County, Alabama. She was probably buried in the Mt. Pleasant Church Cemetery, in the community where she lived her entire life.

Cobb, Melvin

Huston Cobb Jr. interviewed Melvin Cobb, who was 82 years old at the time. Melvin was a son of Tom and Cynthia Foster Cobb. Melvin was the only one of his 15 sibling who was still alive at the time of the interview. Melvin was the grandson of Archie and Candas Cobb.

Archie and Candas

According to the 1910 Colbert County, Alabama, Census, Thomas "Tom" Cobb was born about 1858 to Archie (Archy) and Candas (Candis) Cobb. In the census records, Archie and Candas had the following living in their household:

1. Bedford Cobb, born 1854, Male, Black, farm laborer.
2. Thomas Cobb, born 1858, Male, Black.
3. Henry Cobb, born 1862, Male, Black.
4. Malinda Cobb, born 1863, Female, Black.
5. Caroline "Callie" Cobb, born 1867, Female, Black.
6. Frank Cobb, born 1872, Male, Black.

7.   Mary Cobb, born 1874, Female, Black.

8.   Sally Cobb, born 1876, Female, Black.

9.   Ada Cobb, born 1879, Female, Black.

All the children of Archie and Candas Cobb were born in Alabama.

According to the 1880 Lawrence County, Alabama, Census, Beat 3, Brickville, Township 3, Archie Cobb was born about 1832, and Candas was born about 1833; both were born into slavery. The father and mother of Archie Cobb were slaves born in Virginia. Tom Cobb was born into the slave family of Archie and Candas Cobb just about two years before the start of the Civil War.

Tom and Cindy

On April 28, 1878, Tom Cobb married Cynthia (Synthia) Foster; this information was based on their marriage record. However, Melvin Cobb stated in his interview that Cynthia was a Whiteside, and that she was a sister to Fred Whiteside.

Based on four different census records and the interview of Melvin Cobb, Tom and Cynthia Cobb had 16 children in the family. Some of the census records listed the children of Tom and Cynthia Cobb as Mulatto:

1.   Henry Cobb (1872–?)

2.   Calvin "Cal" Cobb (1874–?)

3.   Henrettia Cobb (1878–?)

4.   Leoagina "Lee" Cobb, Female, (1879–?)

5.   Patsy Cobb (1881–?)

6. Cynthia "Cindy" Cobb (1883–?)

7. Bedford Cobb (1887–?)

8. Mimah "Miny" Cobb (1888–?), who married an Alexander and then Phillip Gardner

9. Emmitt "Emet" Cobb (1889–?)

10. Effie Cobb (1891–?)

11. Ella Cobb (1893–?)

12. Melvin Cobb (1/8/1895–1/?/1984)

13. Frank Cobb (10/7/1896–4/12/1957)

14. Geneva "Jennie" (1899–?)

15. Ethel Cobb (3/10/1900–8/23/1947), who married James Hall. She was buried at Burr Oak Cemetery at Worth in Cook County, Illinois.

16. Lillian "Lillie" Cobb (?–1964)

In the 1920 Colbert County, Alabama, Census, Sheffield, Cynthia Cobb was listed as a 52-year-old Black female; she was the head of the household and widowed. Also listed in her household were the following: Melvin Cobb, Son, Male, 25; Susie Cobb, Granddaughter, Female, 18; Mable Cobb, Granddaughter, Female, 14; and, Herbert Cobb, Grandson, Male, three years four months. At the time of the census, Cynthia was renting her home.

Melvin Cobb said, "I was 15 years old when my daddy Tom Cobb died. My daddy died while living in the Pond Creek or Mt. Olivia. My mother Cynthia Cobb died in 1921."

Frank Cobb

The young Frank Cobb was probably named after his Uncle Frank Cobb. Melvin said, "Frank Cobb was the youngest son of Tom and Cindy Cobb. Frank was taken to Tuscumbia to join the United States Army. He served in World War I."

After Frank Cobb and Misty Howard separated, he married Georgia Smith on March 22, 1914, in Colbert County, Alabama. In 1921, Frank and Georgia Cobb moved to the river and lived near Foster's Mill, which was on Town Creek.

After living on the river, Frank and Georgia eventually moved to Chicago in Cook County, Illinois. On April 12, 1957, Frank Cobb died while his family lived in Illinois. Frank was buried at Restvale Cemetery in Alsip, Illinois.

Bedford Cobb

Bedford Cobb, according to World War I Registration, was born on October 27, 1887, at Town Creek, Alabama. It is interesting that Thomas "Tom" Cobb named one of his sons Bedford, probably after his older brother Bedford. He married Mariah Eggleston, the daughter of James Eggleston and Susan "Susie" Mill.

According to the 1910 Colbert County, Alabama, Census, Brickville, Bedford Cobb was a 23-year-old Mulatto male born about 1887. The following were listed in the household of Bedford: Mariah Cobb, Wife, Female, 22; Reese Cobb, Son, Male, four; Albert Cobb, Son, Male, two; Susan Eggleston, Mother-in-law, Female, 65 (Susan had 12 children with six now living); and Lizzie Miller, Niece, Female, 14.

In 1931, Mariah Eggleston Cobb, wife of Bedford Cobb, died at age 43. She died in Leighton in Colbert County, Alabama. The death record listed her father as James Eggleston and her mother as Susie Mill.

In 1940, Bedford Cobb was living in the household of his cousin, John Lewis Manning. They were living in Election Precinct 1 at Brick in Colbert County, Alabama. Also living in the household of John Manning was Fred Whiteside, who was his 92-year-old father-in-law, and Legie Manning, a 52-year-old female.

Melvin Cobb

On March 22, 1921, Melvin Cobb (1/8/1895–1/1984) married Willie C. Bates in Tuscumbia in Colbert County. She was the daughter of Thornton Bates and Monemia Bell.

Melvin said, "We were married for over 50 years when my wife died. We had four children, but two of our babies died as babies with one being stillborn."

The family of Melvin Cobb first lived in the Bethel Community before moving to Big Nance Creek; the family later moved to the John Henry Bynum Place. After leaving the Bynum Place, the family then moved to the Martin Place. Eventually the family moved back to Bethel Colbert Church Community near Second Street in Colbert County.

During the World War I draft registration for the

military in 1917–1918, Melvin Cobb was living in Knoxville in Knox County, Tennessee. His date of birth was given as January 8, 1895, in Leighton in Colbert County, Alabama.

1930 Census of Melvin

According to the 1930 Colbert County, Alabama, Census, Melvin Cobb was a 35-year-old Black male who first married in at age 26. At the time of the census, Melvin was living in Precinct 17 in Colbert County, and he was listed as head of his household in a home which he was renting.

Also living in the household of Melvin were the following: Willie C. Cobb, Wife, Female, age at first marriage was 22; Emogine Cobb, Daughter, Female, three; Charles T. Cobb, Son, Male, 0; and Herbert Cobb, Nephew, Male, 12. The census stated that Melvin and Willie went to the sixth grade.

Remembrances of Melvin

Melvin described Tom Savage, who was the husband of Momma Callie. Melvin said, "Tom Savage was a yellow man." This probably meant that Tom was Mulatto.

Jerry Cobb married Mariah Miller, sister of Frank Miller. The sister of Mariah Miller married Uncle Bonnie Brown.

Albert Foster married Aunt Callie's daughter. He killed a White man with his pistol.

Death of Melvin and Wille

Melvin Cobb died in January 1984 at the age of 89; his last residence was Sheffield. He and his wife were buried in the Oakwood Cemetery in Sheffield in Colbert County, Alabama.

On January 14, 1970, Mrs. Willie C. Bates Cobb died in Florence in Lauderdale County at age 71. She was buried in the Oakwood Cemetery in Sheffield in Colbert County, Alabama.

Fields, Zela

In 1986, Huston Cobb Jr. interviewed Mrs. Zela Fields when she was 100 years old. At the time of the interview, Zela was in a nursing home, but she still had a remarkable memory.

Zela married Elizah Fields, and they had a daughter, Harris Fields, on August 9, 1909. Harris Fields married Aaron Mitchell, and she died on March 7, 1977, and was buried in the Florence Cemetery in Lauderdale County, Alabama.

Zela Fields said, "In 1886, I was born right here on South Poplar Street in Florence, Alabama. My mother was a slave. My father was also a slave. My mother's master had five brothers: George Ingram, Tom Ingram, Ben Ingram, Lloyd(?) Ingram, and Henry Ingram. My people came out from under slavery."

Ingram Slave Owners

The slave owners mentioned by Zela were found in the Lauderdale County census records. The White family of Ingram brothers owned many Black slaves to work their cotton plantations. Benjamin Ingram owned 25 slaves, George Ingram owned 32 slaves, Joseph Thomas "Tom" Ingram owned 34 slaves, and Henry Ingram owned 49 slaves.

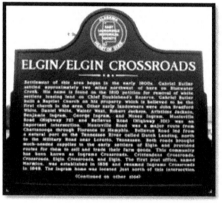

The Ingram home was just north of the intersection that became known as Ingrams Crossroads and later Elgin. The Ingram Family was from Brunswick County, Virginia. Some of the Ingram Family slave owners were buried in the Ingram Cemetery at Thornton Town in Lauderdale County, Alabama.

Benjamin Ingram was born on April 7, 1782, in Brunswick County, Virginia. On April 6, 1808, he married Sarah Mason, who was born on February 10, 1789, in Brunswick County, Virginia. Benjamin and Sarah had the following children:

1. Mary Elizabeth Ingram was born on May 30, 1809, in Brunswick County, Virginia; she married Thomas F. Butler (1802–1851). Mary died on May 10, 1855, in Panola County, Mississippi.

2. Emily E. Ingram was born on July 22, 1810, in Brunswick County, Virginia; she married Walter

M. Haraway. Emily died on January 23, 1867, in Lauderdale County, Alabama.

3. Henry Ingram was born on February 22, 1812, in Brunswick County, Virginia; he died about 1885 in Lauderdale County, Alabama.

4. George Mason Ingram was born on February 23, 1814, in Brunswick County, Virginia; he married Lucy Crittenden (1827–1881). George died on July 19, 1887, in Lauderdale County, Alabama.

5. Sarah Mason Ingram was born on June 22, 1815; she married Thomas Dupree Binford (1816–1888). Sarah died on November 23, 1843.

6. Julia Ann Ingram was born on May 26, 1817, in Lauderdale County, Alabama; she married John Clark Fuqua (1802–1860). Julia died on December 20, 1862, in Lauderdale County, Alabama.

7. Ann M. Ingram was born on April 27, 1819.

8. Octavia Ingram was born on November 1, 1823, in Lauderdale County, Alabama; she married William Henry Crittenden (1815–1854). Octavia died on May 2, 1861, in Lauderdale County, Alabama.

9. Benjamin Ingram Jr. was born on November 1, 1823, in Lauderdale County, Alabama. Benjamin Ingram Jr. was listed in the 1850, 1860, and 1866 census records of Lauderdale County.

10. Joseph Thomas "Tom" Ingram was born on July 17, 1825, in Lauderdale County, Alabama;

he married Mozella Carter (1845–1907). Tom died March 12, 1912, at age 86, and he was buried in the Liberty Cemetery in Rogersville in Lauderdale County, Alabama.

11. Moses Ingram was born on September 15, 1829, in Lauderdale County, Alabama; he married Mary L. Crittenden (1832–1891). Moses died on March 14, 1869, in Lauderdale County, Alabama.

Benjamin died on September 11, 1849, in Lauderdale County, Alabama. Sarah died on September 25, 1852. Benjamin and Sarah were buried in the Ingram Cemetery in Thornton Town in Lauderdale County, Alabama.

American Missionary Association

Zela continued, "I never went to a public school in my life. The American Missionary Association had a little school here called Carpenter High School. They taught in a brick building; since then, that brick school has been demolished. My sister was engaged in teaching there, and she taught me from the time I was in the first grade until probably about the sixth grade."

In 1876, the Carpenter School was for teaching Black

students under the auspices of the American Missionary Society. The school was in the Canaan Subdivision of southwest Florence. Canaan was named in honor of a slave brick mason by the name of Cain Leach. Cain was a slave of John S. Morrow, who owned 10 Black slaves in 1860. On February 22, 1903, Cain died and was buried in the Black section of the Florence City Cemetery.

By April 1897, Miss Mary Lucy Corpier was in charge of the Carpenter School, and she was the first teacher. Mary was a Florence native and graduate of Fisk University.

Zela said, "My sister went to New Jersey to work, and later to an American Missionary Association Mission School at Selma, Alabama. It was named The...School at Burrell, and she went to New York in interest of Florence, and asked they build a school at Florence. At my sister's request, they built Burrell Normal School."

In 1903, Burrell Academy, formerly in Selma, Alabama, was moved to Florence by the American Missionary Association. The school was to serve Black students in first through twelfth grades. In 1937, the Florence City Board of Education assumed its operation and changed the name to Burrell High School. In 1951, the school was moved to Slater Elementary School, and its name was changed to Burrell Slater High School. In 1969, the school closed because of integration.

Zela continued, "My sister did not work for the American Missionary Association any longer, and they ran Burrell School. I did not get to go to Burrell because I went to Fisk University the year it started.

"I went to Fisk University for five years and graduated from what they called the Normal Department, which has since been discontinued. Fisk is a state college where it is now. Normal means teacher; UNA was Florence Normal School or College where students learn to be a teacher."

Church

Zela said the following about church, "During the time that I was working in Colbert County, I did not do very much church work. Initially, I was a member of the First Congregational Church (1875–1939) which was started by the American Missionary Association where Community Church was located on the corner of Mobile and Pine. The Parson's Hall was right next to it. I stayed in that church until the church discontinued.

"When they discontinued their work, the American Missionary Association gave the church and the Pastor's Hall to the community. The county jail used to be right down there, where the Health Department was located. The church and the parsonage area were donated to the City of Florence.

"At least I had learned of the Church of Christ before I went south. Well, I was at the Mother Church of Christ at The Oaks in Colbert County when I heard the first gospel sermon of my life. The minister was a Pastor Hammond out of Corinth, Mississippi; he was a Church of Christ minister. That was the first man I heard preach a gospel sermon and hold it out. That was at Rick's where I grew up.

"You just had a preacher to preach the gospel to you, and when they finished, they offered an invitation. If you wanted to join the church, you go up there and shake his hand. They had a lot of stuff promising when you went in, but you did not have to do anything but go down there and shake hands with the minister.

"In other words, I never have been engaged in all this stuff that most Black folks did. The shouting was just amusing to me. I just like to see them shout some time; I wondered why they do that. When I was working in South Alabama, I learned something of the Church of Christ down there."

Remembrances

Zela said, "I remember some sort of flu epidemic coming through and a lot of people died off. The Nitrate Plant was being built at that time, and all these folk were in here from other places. A lot of people were here working at Plant number two in Sheffield, and a few folks worked at Plant number one. While all those folks were dying, I remember my husband had thirty bodies piled up, but they did not bury them until they tried to establish who they were. He would embalm them and wait for identification.

"I can remember when there were street cars in Sheffield and the Tri Cities. It cost about twenty cents. It was thirty cents from Tuscumbia to Florence.

"At the Sweetwater Plantation, there was a stream that crossed the Old Huntsville Road running right through it called Sweetwater Branch. That is probably why they called it Sweetwater, because the cotton plantation was named after the Sweetwater Creek.

"I remember when the wagon factory was in Florence. A good many people worked at the factory. Mr. Jack Carpenter worked there, but they closed the factory.

"Dr. Hicks was my last Black doctor. Before that time, there was Dr. Simpson, Dr. Town, Dr. Thigpen, and Dr. Long. I also remember Dr. Davis over in Tuscumbia and Dr. Russell. The dentist that we had was Dr. Harding, a cousin of mine."

Zela Fields said, "I do not know if folks are any better than they are right now. There have been days in between that were not so good, but they are very well now."

Anna T. Jeanes

Zela Fields was one of the first Black Jeanes supervisors in Lauderdale County and Colbert County schools. Anna T. Jeanes (April 7, 1822–September 24, 1907) was an American Quaker philanthropist. In 1907, she transferred $1,000,000.00 to the trusteeship of Booker T. Washington and Hollis B. Frissell to be known as "The Fund for Rudimentary Schools for Southern Negroes."

Zela said, "Jeanes was a woman, a Quaker woman,

184

an old maid. And Dr. Booker T. Washington and Dr. Frissell went to Hampton in Virginia. They were trying to solicit some money from her to help in particular schools in Hampton and Tuskegee. They told her of the deplorable condition the country schools were in, and they were trying to solicit her help and were trying to get her interest.

"When they got through she said, 'I would if I could help the little neglected schools.' At that time, they were introduced to keeping the money, and she gave a large sum of money to Tuskegee County and for Macon County. It was the county in which Dr. Frissell was located.

"Miss Anna T. Jeanes gave money for the Jeanes teachers and supervisors to be hired. When she died, she left one million dollars in trust to pay the Jeanes educators. In the meantime, a committee of men was soliciting her wishes, and they were going. She said she wanted it invested in government bonds. They sit down, talked, and talked, and talked, and looked at other things, but she wanted it invested in government bonds.

"Since Miss Jeanes was the donator, they had to ask her about her money. She said that the past 29 years she wanted a solid investment.

"The Great Depression came in 1929–1930. During the depression, the kind of money that had been invested in education was gone.

"I am telling you that Miss Jeanes invested, and she insisted that the Jeanes money be invested in government bonds. When the crash came, her money was solid as the Rock of Gibraltar because she had invested in the United States government bonds."

Teaching Career

Zela Fields said, "I first worked in the Nashville Public Schools as a teacher. I got in by examination in Nashville Public Schools. At that time, Nashville's teachers were having some trouble with examinations. The…were passing in such small numbers that they thought of changing the standards and make it one standard for White people and one for Colored. The Colored people in Nashville did not wish that to be, and they telephoned the Fisk University where I was in school to see if they could send someone down to pass the city examinations. I was selected to go down to take the examination, and out of the 85 that took the test, only 15 of us passed…."

Zela continued, "I taught two years in Nashville before I got married and moved to Sheffield. I did not start teaching in Alabama schools until my children got old enough to leave them.

"When I first started work, I had a man by the name Levi Goode to drive me back and forth for a year. He was working for my husband. My husband was an undertaker; his place of business was on Second Street in Sheffield.

"I later learn how to drive; I had a Ford Sedan, and whatever kind of shift it had. I drove up until the last few years. My last automobile was a brand new V8 Ford, and I sold it in Nashville. I had a Pontiac, a Ford, and another Ford; two Fords and the Pontiac. I sold the last car I had operated just for my use; I did not have any family or anybody to use it."

Zela Fields said, "I worked seven years as a Jeanes

supervisor at Tuscumbia in Colbert County Schools. Johnnie Ester Watkins was also a supervisor; she was in the same kind of work I did.

"Mr. McKey was the Superintendent, and then later, he was defeated by Mr. Robert Hudson; he was superintendent for some time. The reason I left Colbert County was Mr. Hudson did not like the White supervisor. He wanted to get rid of her, and to get rid of her, he had to get rid of me also.

"Mr. Hudson got me a job at Florence in Lauderdale County. I worked three years as a Jeanes supervisor in Lauderdale County, and then I went to South Alabama."

Rosenwald Schools

Zela said, "I don't know near as much about Rosenwald Schools, because when I started work, they had the money and five acres of land for a Cherry Hill school; however, it was not quite enough money to build an adequate school. Mr. McKee, the town supervisor, called me and told me to not tell anyone that he was going to close the Rosenwald School down. He was going to commission it out. He told me that some those folk had better places for their horses and cows than where their children go to school."

Zela continued about the school, "At that time, the students were going to an old, discarded Baptist church, and two women were there. The teacher was Mrs. Hattie Lou Caruthers Ricks, who had been teaching at Cherokee, and Mrs. Caruthers was a supervisor and mother of Mrs. Ricks. And he told me to tell them that he was going to close the school and anything in it. Tell them I said.

"They had a Rosenwald School at Mount Olivia; Pond Creek as they called it, and one at Mount Pleasant. They had a small one at Spring Valley, and they had one teacher at Spring Valley and two teachers at Saint Paul."

Death of Zela Fields

On February 10, 1987, Zela M. Fields died at age 100 in a nursing home. She was buried in Florence City Cemetery in Lauderdale County, Alabama (Find A Grave Memorial Number 156161144).

Hayes, Lucinda Jarmon

In 1985, Mr. Huston Cobb Jr. interviewed Lucinda Jarmon Hayes, who lived in Colbert County, Alabama, all of her life. Lucinda was born on August 19, 1894.

The parents of Lucinda were Albert J. Jarmon (1866–1955) and Cora Hampton (1872–1968). Albert and Cora had six children: Ira Jarmon, who married Lula Mae Vinson; Lucinda Jarmon Hayes, who married Harry Hayes; Elsworth (Jab) Jarmon; Johnny (Shug) Jarmon, who married Emma Kate Bates; Lillie Bell Jarmon Ingram, who married Fred Ingram; and Cornelia Jarmon.

At 16 years old while ironing, Cornelia's clothes caught on fire, and she was severely burned. She lived until the next day and died on December 9, 1915; her body was carried to Mt. Pleasant graveyard in a wagon pulled by mules.

John Jarmon Sr. and Sylvester Eggleston Jarman were the grandparents of Lucinda Jarmon Hayes. Hugh and Albert Eggleston were brothers to Sylvester Eggleston Jarmon. Sylvester was the mother of Albert J. Jarmon, who died on February 20, 1955.

John Jarmon Sr. owned a lot of land north of Leighton in the vicinity of Mt. Pleasant Church, along the County Line Road and Jarman Lane. Much of the land of John Jarmon was purchased by the three brothers of Lucinda Jarmon Hayes—Ira, Jab, and Shug.

White Slave Owners

Cora Hampton, the mother of Lucinda Jarmon Hayes, was thought to be descended from the former Black slaves of Manoah Bostick Hampton Sr. from Stokes County, North Carolina. On January 22, 1825, Dr. John Placibo Hampton was born to Manoah and Cynthia Mitchell Hampton in Lawrence County, Alabama. Their daughter, Mary Mitchell Hampton, was born in North Carolina in 1823. Therefore, the White Hampton family moved from North Carolina to Alabama between 1823 and 1825.

The 1850 census indicates that Manoah Hampton owned 51 Black slaves, and his cotton plantation contained 2,040 acres of land between Leighton and the creek known as Town Creek. According to 1860 census records, Manoah Bostick Hampton Jr. owned 71 slaves; his father had died on February 16, 1858.

Albert J. Jarmon was the father of Lucinda Jarmon Hayes; he was thought to be descended from the former Black slaves of Amos Jarman from Jones County, North

Manoah Bostick Hampton II home in Leighton, AL

Carolina. The cotton plantation home of Amos Jarman was in the Brick Community of present-day Colbert County, Alabama. According to the 1850 census, Amos Jarman owned 50 Black slaves.

Lucinda's Remembrances

Lucinda went to school through the sixth grade in a little log cabin near Mt. Pleasant Church, in front of the graveyard. Her first teacher was Professor John Dobbins. Since the school at Mt. Pleasant did not last but three months, Lucinda went to Hawkins Creek School to get the other three months to make out six months. She walked to school with Arthur Jarmon, Susie Jackson, and Jimmie D. Jackson.

On December 24, 1915, Lucinda Jarmon married Harry Hayes (1892–1963) at Mt. Pleasant Church on the County Line Road in Colbert County, Alabama. Harry and Lucinda Jarmon Hayes had 11 children: Arthur, Lee, Nannie Mae, Lucille, Emily, Earlene, Carl, Thelma, Harry Jr., Oliver, and Gertrude.

In the 1920s, Harry Hayes got a job working on

Wilson Dam, which was the first dam on the Tennessee River in Florence, Alabama. While at work on the dam, Harry was accidently injured when a train car ran over his leg. Because of the severe damage, the doctor had to amputate his leg.

According to the 1940 census records of Colbert County, Alabama, Harry Hayes was 47 years old, and he was the head of his household. His family included his wife, Lusendia Hayes, who was 46; a hired hand by the name of Johnny King Jr., who was 26; a daughter, Lucille Hayes, who was 19; a daughter, Emily Hayes, who was 17; a son, Carl Hayes, who was 15; and a daughter, Earline Hayes, who was 12.

On March 7, 1987, Lucinda Jarmon Hayes died in Sheffield in Colbert County, Alabama. Ms. Lucinda was a few months over 92 years old when she died.

Ingram, Lillie Bell Jarmon

Huston Cobb Jr. interviewed Lillie Bell Jarmon Ingram, the daughter of Albert Jarmon (1866–1955) and Cora Hampton Jarmon (1872–1968). Albert was named after his uncle Albert Eggleston, and his parents were John and Sylvester Eggleston Jarmon. Lillie Bell was a sister to Lucinda Jarmon Hayes, whose interview was included previously.

According to the 1940 Colbert County, Alabama, Census, Albert Jarmon, head of the household, was a 73-year-old Black male born in Alabama about 1867. He was listed as a farm laborer, and he lived in the Town Creek Triangle in Brick Community. Also living in his household was the following: Cora Jarmon was his 67-year-old wife; Elsworth Jarmon was his 38-year-old son; John Jarmon was his 36-year-old son; Emma K. Jarmon was his 34-year-old daughter-in-law; Hightower Jarmon was his 13-year-old grandson; and Cornelias Jarmon was his 12-year-old granddaughter.

In 1940, the Albert Jarmon Family was living next to his brother John and his son Ira Jarmon. John Jarmon was living in household 192, Albert Jarmon was living in household 193, and Ira Jarmon was living in household 194. The all lived in the Brick Community of Colbert County, Alabama.

Ira Jarmon, the oldest son of Albert and Cora and brother to Lillie Bell, was married to Lula Mae Vinson. They had 13 children: Albert, Willie, Fannie Mae, Ira Lee, Levert, Alex, Harold, Pearlean, Margaret, Nazerine, Elsworth, Edna Lee, and Naomi. Ira helped raise his brothers and sisters after his mother Cora died.

Lillie Bell Jarmon Ingram was a member Mt. Pleasant Church. Lillie said, "Mt. Pleasant Church first baptized at the river, and then at Shegog Springs near Brick Church."

Lillie continued, "The school I attended was two stories; John Darby taught downstairs, and Amanda Bailey taught upstairs. The Rosenwald School at Mt. Pleasant had three rooms. Ms. Mattie Johnson from Courtland taught at the Mt. Pleasant Rosenwald School. They bought the property for the school from John Jarmon. After attending Mt. Pleasant, I went to school at Courtland Academy and A&M."

Lillie said, "My momma's momma had a pot for nearly 100 years, we know that. It was her grandmother's pot; her grandmother was Ester Hampton. Her mother got it after Ester died. After her mother died, Aunt Millie Shine, Momma's sister, got the pot. After Aunt Millie died, my momma, Cora Hampton Jarmon, got the pot. Then when momma died, I got it now. It will hold two cans of lard at one time. It is just like it was. It was rusty, and we got it cleaned up."

In 1927, Lillie Bell Jarmon married Fred Ingram. The Black family name of Ingram probably came from the White cotton planters in Lauderdale County. Benjamin, George, Tom, and Henry Ingram were brothers who owned 140 Black slaves.

Fred Ingram retired when he worked at Browns Ferry; he also worked on several TVA dams. He had the following brothers and sisters: Myla Eggleston, Minnie Jarmon, Mark Ingram, Buster Ingram, Milton Ingram, Johnny Ingram, and Julie Ingram.

Lillie Bell Jarmon Ingram died on Monday, February 25, 2002. The funeral was at Mount Pleasant Missionary Baptist Church north of Leighton in Colbert County, Alabama. Lillie was buried in Mount Pleasant Cemetery located in the community where she lived her entire life.

Jarmon, Mamie Johnson

Huston Cobb Jr. interviewed Mamie Johnson Jarmon when she was supposedly 105 years old. She said that she was born on December 12; however, the 1900 census record says she was born in February 1887. The death record of Mamie Johnson Jarmon listed her date of birth as December 18, 1887.

The father of Mamie Johnson was Jerry J. "Gooden" Johnson, the son of Martin Johnson Sr. The mother of Mamie was Chaplin Dickson, daughter of York Dickson Sr. and Irena Dickson.

York Dickson Sr.

York Dickson Sr. was the maternal grandfather of Mamie Johnson Jarmon. Chaplin Dickson Johnson, the mother of Mamie Johnson, had the following siblings: York Dickson Jr. was born about 1835; Rogy Dickson was born about 1841; Josh Dickson was born about 1853; Roseanna "Rosie" Dickson was born about 1852, and she married Phil Whiteside; Irena Dickson was born about 1858, and she married Coleman Johnson; George Dickson was born about 1860; and Mila Dickson was born about 1863.

Mamie said, "My Dickson family lived back over there on the (Tennessee) river. My granddaddy owned a lot of land along the river." Mamie was referring to the land near the mouth of Town Creek and west along the river in present-day Colbert County, Alabama.

Martin Johnson Sr.

Martin Johnson Sr. was the grandfather of Mamie Johnson Jarmon. The 1870 census of Lawrence County, Alabama, Township 3, Range 9 has the following information: Martin Johnson Sr., Black, Male, 52, Alabama; Chany Johnson, Female, 30, Alabama; Martin "Mart" Johnson Jr., Male, 21, Alabama; Narcissa Johnson, Female, 19, Alabama; Catherine Johnson, Female, 17, Alabama; Alice Johnson, Female, 15, Alabama; Coleman "Cole" Johnson, Male, 13, Alabama; Franklin "Frank" Johnson, Male, 11, Alabama; Jerry "Gooden" Johnson (Father of

Mamie Johnson Jarmon), Male, nine, Alabama; Albert Johnson, Male, seven, Alabama; and Lewis Johnson, Male, two, Alabama.

The mother of Jerry J. Johnson was listed as Nar Ciss Johnson in his death record. However, she was not listed in the 1870 census record.

According to the 1870 census, nobody in the household of Martin Johnson Sr. could read or write. The real estate value of Martin Sr. was $400.00, and his personal estate was $700.00.

Jerry J. "Gooden" Johnson

Jerry "Gooden" Johnson was the father of Mamie Johnson Jarmon. According to the 1900 Colbert County, Alabama, Census, Precinct 18 Brickville, Jerry J. "Gooden" Johnson was a 38-year-old Black male. He was born in January 1862 in Alabama, and his parents were born in Alabama. Jerry was married about 1892, and he had been married for eight years. Jerry J. "Gooden" Johnson was renting the property that he was farming.

In the 1900 census, Martha was the wife of Jerry J. "Gooden" Johnson; she was 24 years old and born in February 1876 in Alabama. Martha could read and speak English, but could not write; she had birthed four children and four were still living.

Other family members in 1900 include the following: Mamie Johnson, Daughter, Female, 13, born in February 1887 in Alabama, Cannot read or write; Silvie Johnson, Daughter, Female, seven, born in March 1893 in Alabama; Jerry "Bud" Johnson Jr., Son, Male, five, born in May 1895 in Alabama; Rostan "Royal" Johnson, Son, Male, three, born in Feb 1897 in Alabama; Bennie "Ben" Johnson, Son, Male, two, born in Nov 1898 in Alabama; Otto Whiteside, Hired man, Male, 13, born in Oct 1887 in Alabama.

According to the original census record in 1900, Martha was the second wife of Jerry; she had birthed four living children. Therefore, Mamie, who was 13, could not have been her daughter. Included below is the marriage record of the third wife of Jerry which was the wife after Martha.

By 1910, Mamie Johnson was probably already married; she would have been 23 years old. Mamie was not found in the 1910 census with her father, Jerry J. "Gooden" Johnson.

The 1910 census had Jerry J. Johnson and his family living adjacent to Coleman Johnson, his older brother. Also living within the household of Coleman was the family of his stepdaughter, Rosa Bell Newsome.

In the 1910 Colbert County, Alabama, Census, Brickville, Jerry J. Johnson was a 48-year-old Black male. Living in his household was the following: Martha Johnson, Wife, Female, 38, Alabama; Jerry Johnson Jr., Son, Male, 15, Alabama; Rostan Johnson, Son, Male, 14, Alabama; Silvie Johnson, Daughter, Female, 17, Alabama; Ben Johnson, Son, Male, 12, Alabama; Gazelle Johnson, Daughter, Female, 10, Alabama; Carry May Johnson, Daughter, Female, eight, Alabama; Louie Bell Johnson, Daughter, Female, six, Alabama; Earnest "Ernie" Johnson, Son, Male, four, Alabama; and Albert Johnson, Son, Male, two, Alabama.

The 1910 census stated that Jerry J. "Gooden" Johnson owned his farm but it was mortgaged. The marriage to Martha was his second and the first marriage for Martha; they had been married 18 years at the time of the census.

In the 1910 census, Martha Johnson had nine births and all nine were still living. Martha and all the children are listed as Mulatto. Jerry is listed as Black.

The 1930 Colbert County, Alabama, Census, Brick had the following information: Jerry J. Johnson, Black, Male, 60, Alabama; Mattie Johnson, Wife; Jerry Johnson Jr., Son; Mattie E. Johnson, Daughter; Louie B. Foster, Daughter; Sallie B. Johnson, granddaughter; Curtis Foster, grandson; Pearl Foster, granddaughter; and Mattie L. Foster, granddaughter.

According to the 1830 census, Bennie Johnson, one of Jerry J. Johnson's sons, lived next door to his father. The family of Jerry lived on a farm that he owned. All in the family of Jerry could read and write except his wife Mattie; Mattie was the third wife of Jerry J. Johnson.

On July 19, 1934, Jerry J. Johnson married for the fourth time to Angie Hampton; he was 70 years old and she was 65 years old. Jerry and Angie were married in Colbert County, Alabama, and both were listed as Colored.

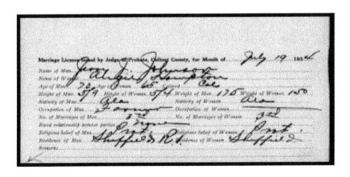

In 1938, Jerry J. "Gooden" Johnson died in Sheffield in Colbert County, Alabama. He was 76 years old at the time of his death. Jerry J. Johnson was buried in the Bethel Colbert Missionary Baptist Cemetery.

Jerry Johnson Jr. was born in 1895 in Colbert County, Alabama. He served in World War I with a lot of other Black soldiers who lived in and around the Town Creek Triangle. He was discharged from the United States Army on February 5, 1919.

Mamie Johnson Jarmon

In her early days, Mamie went to school at Bethel, and she would walk about three to four miles to get to school. From her old home place near the Tennessee River, she and her siblings would walk across the fields to get to school. At the time Mamie was attending Bethel, there were two teachers assigned to teach the students.

Julie was the grandmother to Mamie on her mother's side of the family. There was a pond or hole of water that was called Julie's Pond or Julie's Place; this area was near her old home place.

Mamie heard her folks talk about being under slavery. She was told about her grandmother Julie being sold to a different master.

Mamie Johnson went to church at Bethel Colbert Missionary Baptist Church. Her dad and some of his brothers attended church at Mt. Pleasant.

Mamie said that she had to plow the crops with mules, cut corn stalks for feed, and many other farm chores. She was the oldest child; therefore, she had to help take care of her siblings, do housework, and do farm chores.

There was no mention of her Jarmon husband in the interview. After a search of historical documents, additional information on Mamie Johnson Jarmon's married life could not be found.

Death of Mamie

Mamie Johnson Jarmon was a long-time resident of Leighton in Colbert County, Alabama. Mamie was listed as being 104 years old when she died in May of 1991.

King, Lila Vinson

The story of Lila Vinson King was provided by Huston Cobb Jr.; Lila was a former slave connected to his family by marriage. According to Huston, "Walter James King was the great-grandson of Lila, and he married Mattie Ellen Carter, the sister of my mother Nazareth Carter Cobb. Walter was an overseer for John Fennel; Walter drove the farm truck to carry cotton to the gin and to carry folks to Leighton to Fennel's store to buy groceries."

Lila Vinson was probably a descendant of the Black slaves of Drury Vinson, who was born in Johnson County, North Carolina, on March 4, 1788. He married Mary "Polly" Curtis, who had three Curtis sisters to marry cotton planters that accompanied Drury Vinson to the Leighton area of Colbert County. According to the 1850 slave census, Drury owned 107 Black slaves. Drury died on May 31, 1862, and he was buried in the Vinson Cemetery in Leighton.

Lila Vinson King tells a firsthand account about some of the Fennel slaves; her account was written on September 1, 1948, by Owen L. Crocker. At the time of the interview, Lila was 110 years old, and she was assisted by her son, Fred King. The following is the complete story as told to Owen L. Crocker by Aunt Lila King, assisted by her son Fred, and printed on September 1, 1948.

Lila Vinson King
8/12/1838–1951

Story by Owen L. Crocker

"Lazily winding from the little old southern town of Huntsville, Alabama, the picturesque highway, General Joseph Wheeler, crosses, then follows westward the beautiful Tennessee River. On, or near, this highway are the great Wheeler and Wilson dams, the birthplace of the famed Helen Keller, the home of General Joseph Wheeler of Civil War fame, and the Civil War battlefield of Town Creek. Every mile of the road is full of historical interest; every foot is filled with ancient lore. Here and there are seen old slave towers, relics of by-gone days—grim reminders of humanity in bondage.

Living in a modest little home on this highway between the LaGrange Mountains and the Tennessee River is a former slave, Lila King Vinson, known to the Whites and Blacks alike as 'Aunt Lila.'

Let us turn back the pages of time to that day when the slave woman, Carrie Vinson, persuaded her master to purchase Mose Napper for her to marry. Mose was bought in from North Carolina by the 'Speculators' and sold at Kiddie Carter to the Vinsons. From that marriage were several children, but this story concerns only one, Lila Vinson, born August 12, 1838, one hundred ten years ago.

As Aunt Lila sits in her rocking chair, sewing on her apron and eagerly answering your questions, you are amazed at her active mind, her firm and steady voice, as she rethreads her needle without the aid of glasses. Her memory is so clear that she recalls one hundred years ago as if it were only yesterday. Many people only half her age are not so well preserved. Four years ago she fell and broke her leg while trying to get the mule out of the garden, but the cast itched so badly that she tore it off causing her leg to become twisted, which permits her to only hobble around.

The first twenty-seven years of her life were spent in slavery along with approximately one hundred others on the same place. Good mules on the farms were treated with more consideration, given better things to eat, and brought more money in a trade. Every slave was kept busy from daylight to dark and later, plowing the fields, picking cotton, tending the cattle, and the various tasks around the farms. Overseers made sure that these tasks were performed, or that severe punishment was inflicted.

Uncle Bust King, an old and feeble slave, was made to pick cotton down in the swamps where the water was knee deep. This was done by the light of pine torches. He fell out—with pneumonia. The overseer whipped him and made him go back to work, and to die. He had just 'fessed' religion, and his last words were 'Jesus, draft this cloud back, for such as these won't do to burn.' The slaves made a pine box, painted it black with soot and buried him.

As a very small child Lila was made to knit. She was made to stand on one foot behind her mistress for hours at a time and if she once put her raised foot down, she got a whipping. She also had to rake leaves and help haul them off to the farms. Sometimes the piles of leaves would be almost as high as the shade trees. Invariably, she helped load up the wagons next day with leaves…A long house was used to take the babies to while the women were working in the fields. Very old, feeble women fed (slopped) the babies. Sometimes the mothers would moan and cry for their babies, but the overseers would whip them and make them go on to work. Oft times the mothers were sold or traded, leaving the babies in the 'slop' house.

'Aunt Lila' clearly remembers slave George Fennel. Because of a little infraction of a rule, George had a stick run under his knees, his arms tied around it, kicked over, and whipped with a rawhide whip until he passed out, but they kept on beating him. His body was a solid mass of bloody meat, his back 'laid open' in slits. And there was Mae Hunter's son who was tied over a barrel, and ridden with spurs like a horse.

Then there was old George who tried to run away. They 'sicked' the blood hounds on him. (Usually the dogs tore the slaves up and ate them.) Old George carried a grass scythe with him, and when the dogs cornered him, he began to swing the blade. 'Dog legs, heads, and guts shore was scattered around there.' The overseers came up on him, carried him back to the house and whipped him.

Sometimes, Lila would go with the boys to haul water from the Blue Hole, a large bottomless, beautiful pool. Aunt Timmey's son backed the wagon into this pool and was never seen again. This same pool is used to this day for watering the stock in the pasture.

A note (or pass) was required for any slave to leave the place for any reason. To leave without this pass meant a sure whipping. This rule was true in every case, even to church, to the next farm, or wherever it might be. Many slaves would live and die on the place, unless traded or sold, without ever having been one mile off the premises.

One of 'Aunt Lila's' first whippings was administered

to her when she was old enough to walk good. She was dropping corn in the field, planting the check system, but she was dropping it where it would later have been plowed up.

The slaves lived in small stalls, just room enough for a bed, a fireplace on which to cook, and a table. This was the home of one family. Hogs were killed and distributed among them. 'Aunt Lila' remembers that the insides of the hogs were eaten just as they were because, in her words, 'The Black folks were no better that the hogs they ate.'

Snuff was made by grinding the dried tobacco leaves in the coffee mill, chewing tobacco was made by putting sorghum molasses between several layers of tobacco leaves, putting them under the fence rails to press, and letting them stay there for some time.

One of the most cruel taskmasters was Granville Pillars who married Aunt Lila's mistress, Miss Lucy. His delight was to torture everybody—even his wife, actually beating her and literally throwing her across the room by the hair on her head. He 'sicked' the dogs on the slave girls and was amused when the dog 'Lela' chewed parts of the flesh from their bodies. He shot and killed 'Aunt Lila's' brother, Tuskee, for coming over on his property hunting a cow. The KKK, however, put an end to his cruelty by killing him, shooting his tongue off first.

In the 1850's, the slaves heard and passed on the word that they would be freed. There arose a mighty controversy. The cry was heard 'You shall be free,' but another was, 'You shan't be free.' This spread like wild fire, and then it happened—the great Civil War of 1861–1865.

The North against the South, father against son, brother against brother—the fought each other in the bloodiest war this country had ever seen. There was not first aid to the wounded, you lay where you were hit, twisted, cried, and suffered until you died.

Battles were fought all along the Joe Wheeler Highway. Markers now depict each battle. Camps were pitched on the place of 'Aunt Lila King's' folks. 'Aunt Lila' was 'thinking herself a grown woman then'—eighty-eight years ago. Her mother died before peace was made some years later.

The Yankees swept down from the North pillaging, burning, and taking everything. The Whites and colored alike fled to the hills until the army passed over, then more would come. The people buried all valuables—tar, grease, money, syrup, and meat. The Yankees went into the smoke houses and threw hams out to the naked colored children. Hood's army was after the Yankees at Town Creek. The Yankees burned the bridge, so the Confederates cut down a large tree across the small creek to use as a foot log (bridge). That log is still to be seen lying about a foot under the water—hard as a rock—petrified. Here the Battle of Town Creek was fought—a bloody, an awful battle.

The Yankees burned LaGrange Academy, a large school on top of the mountain where 'Aunt Lila' waited on the tables. Miss Hastings tended the school (and drank three cups of coffee each meal). During the burning everybody carried off everything they could find. One slave carried off a sack full of stuff. When he got down to the foot of the mountain, he and 'Aunt Lila' found it to be a sack of broken pitchers. She had carried off a little red chair.

After the Yankees had taken everything, 'Aunt Lila' and the others used leaves to wrap the food in before covering it with ashes to cook it. Times were hard for all. To add to the confusion, wolves came down from the mountains…to feed on the fresh killed meat, whether it was pigs, horses, dogs, or soldiers.

Uncle Billy Yancy was a Negro preacher who held his meetings under brush arbors. His folks would get filled up with religion and go into wild fits. Old Martha Franks became so full of religion that she danced around and broke her leg. The usual method of marrying the slaves was to simply make the man and woman hold hands and jump over a broom stick, and they became man and wife. 'Aunt Lila,' however, met Louie King in the edge of the woods, they got a marriage license at Courtland and were married. She was permitted to move her bed that night. She and Louie had nineteen children before he died in 1911 at the age of seventy-four.

Lila's children are: Living: Lue Belle, Zella, Charity, Charles, Fred (youngest—age 51, July 31, 1948). Dead: Cherry (oldest—died 1920, age 57), Ross, Jackson, Louise, Bowlin, Emma, Fanny, Susan, Louie, Mary, Addie, and one set of triplets unnamed. At a family reunion in 1911, there were sixty-three grandchildren. In 1941, there were forty-nine great grand children. No count has been taken since then.

Aunt Lila sits on her porch basking in the warm sun, she recalls over one hundred years—a full century—of life at its worst to a now relative life of ease. As she watches her children's, children's, children grow up free to go and come at will, she remembers those days of slavery—human bondage—when one had to have a pass to go to the adjoining farm. Those horrible wars, beatings, and mutilated bodies that we only read about are very real, very actual, to 'Aunt Lila.' But she is happy, happy because she has so many friends, both Black and White, who bring her gifts almost daily. Her days are filled with the joy of living. Let's hope she has a lot more of them."

Aunt Lila Conclusion

Aunt Lila's home was on County Highway 64 about one mile northeast of Cotton Town Church and about a half mile south of new Highway 20 in Colbert County, Alabama. When Huston Cobb's Aunt Mattie Ellen Carter married Walter James King, she moved in the house with Walter and his grandmother, Lila Vinson King, a former slave.

Within one mile of Aunt Lila Vinson King's old home place are two King Cemeteries. A Black King Cemetery can only be identified by field stones and a few markers which identify the graves of former slaves. The White King Cemetery is well kept and not far from the creek of Town Creek; graves are marked with large marble monuments to their family members. These White King Family members were some of the first families to own slaves in the Town Creek Triangle.

King, Mattie Ellen Carter

On April 13, 1986, Huston Cobb Jr. interviewed his aunt, Ms. Mattie Ellen Carter King. Mattie Ellen Carter was the sister to Nazareth Carter Cobb, the mother of Huston Cobb Jr. Mattie Ellen married Walter James King, who was the great-grandson of Lila Vinson King.

The parents of Mattie Ellen Carter were Tracy Carter and Fannie Johnson Carter. Tracy and Fannie had six girls and three boys: Nazarene, Carl Anthony, Willie Dean, Caroline, Mary Alice, Mattie Ellen, Anneline, Jimmy, and Odesa.

Walter James King and Mattie Ellen Carter

Ms. Ellen said, "My grandmother was Caroline. We called her Mama Caroline, that's what we called her, and I used to give her medicine. I remember fixing chicken feed for her all the time when we was small. Now our home was down on the branch right across from grandpa's old house. We all would go on down, cross a little stream of water. It was a ditch, and we had to come up the hill to the house with water all the time. We had to come up through grandpa's orchard and through the locked gate to get water in the evenings and mornings; it was a great big locked gate. I remember my Mama Caroline, that's what we called her, and she would always have us beat corn in the mornings and in the evenings for her chickens. She had lots of chickens to feed. Well, we would go to draw water, and we'd have to stop and beat corn. We beat up so much corn for the chickens for the next day before we could go back home."

Mama Caroline was the great-grandmother of Huston Cobb Jr.; she married Martin Johnson Jr. Caroline Carter was the Mulatto daughter of Viney, a Black slave.

Ellen continued, "I remember Grandpa Martin well. He was a big, strong, healthy man. He looked like he weighed almost 300 pounds to me. He was big and tall, but he wasn't fat. Grandpa had the prettiest white teeth. Had never had a toothache or never had nothing done to his teeth. I remember that cause I said I had always wished for pretty teeth. His teeth are just like somebody had just got new ones. He had never had anything done to his mouth, and never had any decayed teeth or nothing.

"After Mama Caroline died, Grandpa Martin stayed there in his house. We used to go around there and stay because Mama Caroline's baby sister was living out there in a house close to Grandpa. Her house was close to the barn and the road.

"Grandpa Martin had three houses on his place that I know and that was Uncle Bud's house. It was the prettiest white house I ever seen. It was over on a hill. It had the biggest lighting rods with an iron horse wind vane. You could go around that beautiful house, and you could tell which way the wind was blowing by watching that horse on Bud's house. His house was way over in the field going towards the creek, and that part of the land run down straight back to the creek. We used to play down there.

"Papa Martin's house and Mama Caroline's house was where we were all born. It was a white house with green shutters and a long porch with white beautiful post across the porch. I well remember that house.

"Mama Caroline died first long before Papa Martin. She died about two months after my brother Willie Dean died. My brother Willie Dean and my sister Mary Alice died close together. My sister Mary Alice was carrying me up to my Mama Caroline's house while they were getting ready to bury Willie Dean, and she died. That is all I remember of Mary Alice.

"Yep, I remember that real well, but I just can't picture nothing. It was like a dream, but I remember Mary Alice carrying me up there and telling me we had to go up there so they could get ready for the funeral. There was two years difference in all of us almost, and it was almost five between me and my sister Caroline.

"When we left the home place of Grandpa Martin and Mama Caroline, we moved to Second Street. Grandpa eventually moved with us because he could not see after himself. Mama had to go down and see about him so often. Mama got to where she was not able to go down and see about him all the time. Mama moved him with us and that is why we had the problem with the farm. We had to get Grandpa all the time because he would slip off and go down in the weeds, down below our barn."

Long, Nellie M. Ricks

In 1982, Huston Cobb Jr. interviewed Nellie M. Long; she was born on June 10, 1904, in Sheffield in Colbert

County, Alabama. Nellie was the daughter of Grant Ricks Sr. (9/16/1862–1938), who was 41 at her birth, and Mary Freeman (10/9/1873–1948), who was 30 when Nellie was born.

Grant Ricks descended from the Black slaves of Abraham Ricks of The Oaks Plantation; he was the son of Parson George Ricks. Mary Freeman Ricks, the wife of Grant, probably descended from the Black slaves of Jane M. Freeman, who owned 20 slaves according to the 1860 Colbert County, Alabama, Census.

Grant and Mary Freeman Ricks had 13 children: Louvenia Ricks (1886–1994), Mary Ricks (1886–1994), Ethel R. Ricks (1888–1988), John Bell Ricks (1890–1965), Percy E. Ricks Sr. (1891–1979), Lavana Ricks (1892), McKinley Ricks (1896–1956), Grant Ricks Jr. (1898–1962), Ellis Ricks (1903–1984), Nellie Mae Ricks (1904–1998), Mattie Lee Ricks (1905–1926), Fred Ricks Sr. (1907–1972), and Beatrice R. Ricks (1912–1990).

At the time of the interview, Nellie said, "I now reside at the address of 801 East 19th Street, Sheffield. On October 22, 1922, I married Harry Winston Long Sr. (1/31/1891–3/10/1940); he had three brothers and two sisters. After we got married, we first lived in front of a cemetery in Sheffield, Alabama, on Jackson Highway, and from there, we moved to where I now live; I have lived here 63 years."

Harry and Nellie M. Long had two sons and seven daughters: Sally Mae Long Taylor (1923–1970), Virginia Minerva Long Brock (1924–1995), Thelma Long (1926–1966), Ernestine Long (1927–1931), Beatrice Nell Long

(1928–1996), Isaiah "Zeke" Long (1930–2008), Harry "Bone" Winston Long Jr. (1932–1999), Marilyn Long Crawford (1934–2009), and Doris Long (1936–2011).

Nellie said, "Virginia lives in Detroit; she married Frank Brock. They have a son, Frank Jr., who is a supervisor for Ford Motor Company."

Doris Long was the only child of Nellie M. Long to live with her at the time of the interview. Doris Long said, "I'm Nellie Long's daughter. I'm the supervisor of the instructions at the Board of Education, and at this time, we still have records of students that attended the church school. Many people come to get their birth certificates, birth dates, social security, and other information, and all of the students that attended that school is on the registry in the Department of the Board of Education."

Nellie said, "My grandfather was George Ricks, and he was given this name by Abraham Ricks. He was born in Jamestown, Virginia, and he was brought to Spring Valley. His folks came here from Liberia."

Nellie continued, "The place where Abraham Ricks once lived is called The Oaks. The things that remind me of where my Grandfather George lived is the cemetery and the church. The cemetery is on 53 acres of land, and the first property known to be owned by a colored man in North Alabama. He earned his money to buy this land by picking and working a cotton patch on a Saturday evening and picking it by the moonlight. After he was free, he bought three hundred acres of land and built a church house on it. He deeded one acre to the church which is now the Church of Christ down until this day. This church was the first or one of the first Black Church of Christ in Alabama.

"Preston Taylor baptized Grandfather George Ricks. Preston was at Alexander Campbell's crusades that was coming down through here carrying the gospel when Alexander Campbell first came to America and established the church in America. Preston Taylor was the only one to baptize Black folks. He's the only one that's known to me. Out of knowing him, Preston Taylor came through here and this is how the Ricks got to be members of the Church of Christ. Umm, I understand that they also baptized during this time, or were they already members. All of the masters, grandfathers, Abraham Ricks, him and his family were members of the Church of Christ in Spring Valley, and that church is still there.

"The church at The Oaks was the first Church of Christ known to be owned in North Alabama by a Black man. It was built by George Ricks, my grandfather, and he also preached to his people at this church.

"They called my grandfather Pastor George Ricks because he preached to the people. He did not confine his preaching to this area; he went far down in South Alabama and Mississippi preaching the gospel. The church of Corinth, Mississippi, came from his church.

"At the time of his death in 1908, I was four years old. He was buried in the cemetery at The Oaks; he gave the cemetery to the people after slavery. They didn't have no burial ground. He gave three acres to everybody of colored race to be buried in this cemetery. No one has ever paid for a grave and this cemetery is still in use and the ones that use it now have never paid for a grave until this day. This is probably the only cemetery in the area that they don't pay.

"Percy Ricks had Brother Keegle to come from here. He was brother Keegle's brother-in-law; they married sisters. Brother Keegle had come down in this area in these parts I guess it was around 1917 or 1916 something like that, and he came down and preached."

Nellie said, "Brother Hannah was the minister at the church until about 1930. His home was in Corinth. He came up and preached every 4th Sunday at Ricks Church. Pastor Mullens, they call him, he was the grandfather of Elvin Mullens. Now, I don't know where he was from. Elvin Mulley was one of the members in Sheffield at one time, and that was his grandfather.

"The church was also used as a school building for the people that lived in that vicinity at that time. I went to that school, and that was where I got my education from. It was a one-room school, and three of the grandchildren of George Ricks taught there, and it continued to be a school until about 1939."

Nellie said, "George Ricks was the father of seven children, according to my knowledge. My father was Grant Ricks, and he had eleven children. There are five of us still alive, four girls and one boy by the name of Ellis Ricks. Bonnie lives in Sheffield, and she is a member of the church of Christ, at the age of 96 and still praising. According to my knowledge, all of my brothers and sisters are members of the Church of Christ."

Nellie said, "I moved away from this house twice; the first time I moved away was during the life of my husband. We moved up to his father's home after father was deceased and he was planning on taking care of younger sisters and brothers. He moved up here to take care of them, and he died there on March 10, 1940. After his death, I lived there for two years and moved back here. In 1949, I moved to Nashville, Tennessee. I carried five children with me at that time. I moved there and put all of these five children through the state college in Tennessee.

"Well I'm the grandmother of 27 grandchildren, and out of that 27, I don't have the true knowledge of what the children have done naturally. In those 27, just about all of them attended state college in Nashville. Two of my grandchildren have a doctor's degree in Dentistry; one has an office in Sheffield.

"In 1957, I moved back here from Nashville. After moving back home to Sheffield, I raised a grandson, which is Linus. I sent him to David Lipscomb College, and he finished there; he is now working with the Reynold's Metal Company."

Nellie said, "I raised six children that were my niece's children; her name was Vera Sneed. Vera got burned to death and left six children. I claimed custodian over those children because their father was unable; he was 100% disability. The government empowered me as their custodian."

Nellie said, "When I moved back here in 1957 to Sheffield, I found the Cobb family and the Shelton family attended church. They had obeyed the gospel and were attending service at the Mainfield Street Church of Christ in Sheffield.

"I had two brothers, Percy Ricks and Fred Ricks, they are both dead. Percy was a preacher; he preached along the way. In 1919, I went to school in Tuscumbia in Junior High, and I lived with Percy, and he married in August of 1919.

"Percy came home from the army. At the time when I was living with him in Tuscumbia, the Lord established the Church of Christ there. So his (Percy) wife, being a member of the church in Corinth, Mississippi, I heard her crying all night one night, but could not recognize what she was crying about. But, I found out she was crying because Percy had left to go to a Baptist church on Sunday evening and she told him that where there was enough people living in Tuscumbia members of the Church of Christ will get together and get the church started. He did that, and the first service they had together was at a high school. He got to serve eleven years in sixth-grade rooms at the high school, and that's where we had service on Sunday. I was with him and his wife when he walked in the door of Tuscumbia to start a church, because he built this church in 1922; that is what is on the cornerstone. Some of the members think that is when it started, but it started in 1919; in 1922, he had this building completed.

"Percy built the church all by himself, wasn't a man there to help him. And after they found out that this was a Church of Christ, they started trying to have service. Percy went right behind the Methodist church over there and that's where he attended service until he bought this lot where the Church of Christ is now, and he put a tent on it until he got the building built. He also built the church in Cherokee. In all them churches down there, he had a hand in getting them established. The church in Sheffield, it was him that called a brother to come to Sheffield and start a meeting here. In 1926 at this meeting, six couples obeyed the Gospel, including Brother Ed Nurhall and Brother Terry Tomlinson, Brother Acres and his wife, and Brother Brown and his wife, and from there the church started in Sheffield and had meetings in Brother Ed Nurhall's home.

"Percy Ricks also had people to come to Florence, but I can't remember the year they had a church that started in Florence. I remember the year about Sheffield though, and started a meeting over there."

On December 26, 1998, Nellie Mae Ricks Long died in Sheffield in Colbert County, Alabama, at the age of 94. Harry and Nellie Ricks Long were buried in the George Ricks Cemetery at The Oaks Plantation site south of Leighton in Colbert County, Alabama.

Mullens, Richard "Dice"

Huston Cobb Jr. interviewed Richard "Dice" Mullens, who said at the time that he was 86 years old. The father of Dice was John Mullens, and his mother was Fannie Vinson.

John Mullens was born in 1879, and he died on January 19, 1954. The father of John Mullens was George Granville Spangler (1846–1986). The mother of John was Sallie Mullens (1849–1896).

The parents of John Mullens were born into slavery in Lawrence (Colbert) County, Alabama. The Black family of Mullens probably got their family name from the White cotton planters named Mullins. In the 1850 Lawrence County, Alabama Census, Gabriel, James H., and William Mullins owned 63 Black slaves.

John and Fannie Vinson Mullens had seven children who were born four miles from Leighton:
1. Vashti Mullens was born in 1904.
2. Lester "Buster" Mullens was born in 1905.
3. Richard "Dice" Mullens was born on December 3, 1905.
4. Rebecca was born in 1909.
5. Ella D. Mullens was born in 1911, and she died in 2003.
6. Annie V. Mullens was born in 1914.
7. Weller L. Mullens was born in 1915, and she died in 2008.

According to the 1920 Colbert County, Alabama, Census, Leighton Precinct 11, Household 193, John Mullens was a 44-year-old Mulatto male farmer who was renting his home. He could read and write. Also in the household were the following: Fannie Mullens, Wife, Female, Mulatto, 38; Vashti Mullens, Daughter, Female, Mulatto, 16; Lester Mullens, Son, Male, Mulatto, 15; Richard Mullens, Son, Male, Mulatto, 14; Rebecca Mullens, Daughter, Female, Mulatto, 11; Ella D. Mullens, Daughter, Female, Mulatto, eight; Annie V. Mullens, Daughter, Female, Mulatto, six; and Weller L. Mullens, Daughter, Female, Mulatto, four.

At the time of the interview, Dice said, "I lived in Detroit for 14 years. I lived in Chicago for 30 years. My brother Buster never went anywhere, but he came to Chicago to see me. I have been back home in Alabama for 23 years."

Dice continued, "I lived about four miles from

Leighton at a place called Bob Canyon. My old home place was near Mount New Home Baptist Church. My mother was Fannie Vinson; she was raised up out there not far from Mount New Home Church. My mother was a sister to Aunt Ray, Aunt Sue, Aunt Martha, Aunt Lula Mae, and Aunt Rachel."

Mount New Home Baptist Church is on Cotton Town Road about one mile east of the County Line Road. The church is about four miles southeast of Leighton, Alabama, in present-day Colbert County.

Dice said, "My father was John Mullens. His brothers were Ed Mullens, Jay Mullens, Willie Mullens, and Jake Mullens. His five sisters were Molly, Chloe, Rebecca Bates, Pearl Hankins, and Mattie Hood. Pearl Mullens Hankins had two sons—Carl and Sammy."

Dice said, "I left Leighton and went north, and I had 39 cents. It took a week to get to St. Louis; I was hoboing on trains. I had quite a few people in St. Louis, and I got job in a bottle factory and worked one week. The man paid me off, and I wanted to go to Detroit. That day, I caught a freight, and next day, I was in Detroit."

Dice continued, "As far as hoboing, there is not a railroad in the United States that I have not been on. There is not a big city in the United States that I have not been in, and I have not bought but three tickets in my life; hoboed over all of them.

"There will be a Hobo Convention in Knoxville, Tennessee. They have a prize for the oldest Hoboer, and a prize for the name of the states and railroads going from city to city and know them by heart; they have a big prize for him. A colored fellow won it last year down at Louisiana, and he was not but 74. Now me being 86, I might be the oldest Hoboer in the United States."

Dice said, "The Griffin Pruitt children included Gordon Pruitt, Mammoth Pruitt, Edmon Hill (sister), and William Pruitt. Griffin had a brother named Price. Old man Richard Pruitt house was at the corner of County Line Road and new Hwy 20. He had a son named Gordon."

On February 11, 1999, Richard "Dice" Mullens died at Moulton in Lawrence County, Alabama. He was 93 years old, but his gravesite is unknown.

Newsome, Rosa Belle

Huston Cobb Jr. interviewed Rosa Belle Newsome; at the time, she was in her late 80s. According to the Social Security records, Rosa Belle Newsome was born on August 4, 1891.

The Black family name of Newsome probably came from the White cotton plantation owner by the name of Whitmill R. Newsome. According to the 1860 Franklin (Colbert) County, Alabama, Census, Whitmill Newsome owned 82 Black slaves.

The mother of Rosa Belle Newsome was Irena Dickson. The Black family name of Dickson probably came from the White plantation owner by the name of William Dickson. According to the 1860 Colbert County slave census, William Dickson owned 83 Black slaves.

York Dickson

The father of Irena was York Dickson (Dixon) Sr., and her mother was also named Irena. York Dickson Sr. and his wife, Irena Dickson, were born into slavery. After the Civil War, York owned a lot of land along the Tennessee River near the Bethel Colbert Church Community in Colbert County, Alabama.

According to the 1870 Lawrence (Colbert) County, Alabama, Census, Township 3 Range 9, the following records were as follows: York Dickson Sr., Male, Black, 50 (Actually 55 years old), Estimated Birth Year 1820 (Date of birth was June 1815), Alabama, Real Estate Value $1400.00, Personal Estate Value $700.00; Irena Dickson, Wife, Female, 50, Alabama; Rogy Dickson, Male, 29, Alabama; Josh Dickson, Male, 17, Alabama; Roseanna Dickson, Female, 18, Alabama; Irena Dickson, Female, 12, Alabama; George Dickson, Male, 10, Alabama; and Mila Dickson, Female, seven, Alabama. Roseanna "Rosie" Dickson married Phil Whiteside.

According to the 1870 Colbert County, Alabama, Census, Township 3 Range 11, the records were as follows: York Dickson Jr., Male, Black, 35, Birth Year (Estimated) 1835, Alabama, Cannot read or write, Value of personal Estate $200.00, Farm Laborer; Virginia Dickson, Female, 23, Virginia, Keeping House, Cannot read or write; Herman Dickson, Male, four, Alabama; and James Dickson, Male, four months old, Alabama.

On May 31, 1872, York Dickson Sr. married Malinda Cobb in Lawrence County, Alabama. York and Malinda Cobb Dickson did not have any surviving children.

The following records were found in the 1900 Colbert County, Alabama, Census, Brickville, Precinct 18, Household 24: York Dixon Sr., Male, Black, 85, Ford City, Birth Date Jun 1815, Tennessee, Married, Years Married 27, Head of Household, Father's Birthplace Tennessee, Mother's Birthplace North Carolina; Malinda Dixon, Wife, Female, 71, Alabama, number of births 1, number of children living 0, Birth December 1829; and Andrew Shaw, Male, 17, Alabama. At the time of the census, York Dickson was living next door to Coleman Johnson, where Rosa Belle Newsome lived.

A Colbert County death record listed York Dickson Sr. dying on August 1, 1908. The burial site of York Dickson was not available.

Coleman Johnson

Since her mother, Irena, was born in 1858 and her stepdad was born in 1856, they were both born into slavery. By 1900, her mother, Irena, had married Coleman Johnson, the son of Martin Johnson Sr. It appears that Irena Dickson had first married a Newsome, and she had two girls—Stalla and Rosa Belle—by Newsome.

The following information was found in the 1900 Colbert County, Alabama, Census, Brickville, Precinct 18: Coleman Johnson, Head, Male, Black, 44, Alabama; Irena Dickson Johnson, Wife, Female, Black, 41, Alabama; Stalla Newsome, Stepdaughter, Female, Black, 12, Alabama; Rosa Newsome, Stepdaughter, Female, Black, nine, Alabama; York Johnson, Son, Male, Black, four, Alabama; John Johnson, Son, Male, Black, two, Alabama. York Johnson was named after his grandfather, who was York Dickson.

The 1910 Colbert County, Alabama, Census, Brickville, was as follows: Coleman Johnson, Black, Male, 54, Married, born in 1856 in Alabama; Irena Johnson, Wife, Female, 48, Alabama; York Johnson, Son, Male, 14, Alabama; John Johnson, Son, Male, 12, Alabama; Jacob Johnson, Son, Male, nine, Alabama; Rosa Bell Newsom, Stepdaughter, Female, 19, Alabama; and William Newsome, Step-grandchild, Male, two, Alabama.

According to the marriage records of Colbert County, Alabama, on December 30, 1914, Rosa Belle Newsome married George Hampton. At the time of their marriage, Rosa Belle Newsome was 23 years old.

By the 1920 census, Rosa Belle Newsome was back in the household with her mother Irena and her stepfather Coleman Johnson. It was not known if George Hampton died or Rosa Belle Newsome left him and kept her maiden name. At the time of the census, Rosa Belle had her two boys.

The 1920 Colbert County, Alabama, Census, Brick, Precinct 1, Household 122 had the following information: Rosabell Johnson (Rosa Belle Newsome), Female, Black, Single, 27, Relationship to Head Daughter (Step Daughter); Coleman Johnson, Father (Step Father), Male, 63, Birth Year (Estimated) 1857, Alabama, Married, Black, Head of Household; Irena Johnson, Mother; York Johnson, Brother (Half Brother); Jacob Johnson, Brother (Half Brother); Marcellus Johnson (Newsome), grandson (Step Grandson), five; Robert Lee Johnson (Newsome), grandson (Step Grandson), three; and William Newsom, grandson, 10.

In 1920, the census taker listed Rosa Belle Newsome and her two sons as Johnson; however, they went by the name Newsome. The 1920 census also listed William Newsome as a 10-year-old grandson of Coleman Johnson. It was not clear how William was listed as a grandson.

Rosa Bell Newsome said that she only had two children: Marsel Newsome and Robert Lee Newsome. The parents of Robert Lee Newsome Sr. were listed in his marriage records as Nathan Fuqua, his father, and Rosa Belle Newsome, his mother.

Death of Rosa Belle

According to the United States Social Security Death Index, Rosa Belle Newsome died in February 1984 at the age of 93. At the time of her death, Rosa was living in Sheffield in Colbert County, Alabama.

Marcella Newsome

According to the 1940 Colbert County, Alabama, Census, Marsel Newsome was living in the household of Houston Cobb Sr. Marsel was 25 years old and married at the time of the census. It appears that his wife was Geneva, and she was 21 years old.

Based on the 1940 census record, Marsel was born about 1915, and his wife Geneva was born about 1919. There were two children with Marsel and Geneva as follows: Gladys M. Newsome, who was a four-year-old Black female, and Rosella Newsome, who was a three-year-old Black female. All the members of the Marsel Newsome Family were listed as cousins of Houston Cobb Sr., and all were born in Alabama.

Robert Lee Newsome Sr.

On March 12, 1940, Robert Lee Newsome Sr. married Lucille Bates in Colbert County, Alabama; Robert was 24 and Lucille was 18. The parents of Lucille Bates were Green Bates and Gazell Johnson. Lucille was a sister to Percy Bates.

Robert Lee Newsome Jr. was the son of Robert Lee Newsome Sr. and Lucille Bates Newsome. He was born on March 5, 1950, and died on January 23, 2019. Robert Jr. had the following siblings:

Robert Lee Newsome Jr.

Edward Newsome, Derrick Newsome, Rosie L. Freeman, Josephine Bankhead, Alfshteen Ricks, Jeraldine Phillips, Betty Tiggs, Esther Horrison, and Wanda Goodloe.

Pearsall, Ophelia Hill

About 1979, Huston Cobb Jr. interviewed Ophelia Hill Pearsall; she was born on July 19, 1894. At the time of the interview, Ophelia was 85 years old.

Family of Ophelia

The parents of Ophelia were Lloyd Hill and Nancy Hampton. The brothers of Lloyd Hill were Logan Hill, Emmitt Hill, Bowling Hill, and Charlie Hill.

Lloyd Hill and Nancy Hampton Hill had the following children: Ophelia Hill, LeAnna Hill Stewart,

Christine Hill Smith, Lucille Hill Stanton, Lewis Hill, Henry Hill, Emmitt Hill, and Stephen Hill. Henry and Emmitt Hill lived in Chicago, Illinois, and Lewis lived in Detroit, Michigan. Lucille lived in Chattanooga, Tennessee, and LeAnna lived in Richmond, Indiana.

School

Olivia said, "I went to school at Mt. Olivia or Pond Creek. Some of the Colored kids I attended school with were the children of Lewis Long. I walked to school with Annie, Will, and Harry Long."

Mt. Olivia (Mount Olivious) School was located at the junction of the Ford Road and Second Street in Colbert County. The school was located in the community that was also known as Listerhill or Pond Creek. Mt. Olivia was about three miles southwest of Hawkins Creek School.

Hawkins Creek School was in the Hawkins Creek Community some two miles west of Ford City. The school was south of the Tennessee River about two miles on Byler's Old Turnpike Road, also known as the Bainbridge Road. It was just about a half mile south of the junction of the River Road and Bainbridge Road, and was located on the west side of the road in Colbert County, Alabama.

Olivia continued, "The ferry which crossed the Tennessee River north of where I grew up was known as Bainbridge. The area to the south along Bainbridge Road was known as Cunningham Bottoms. Robert Cunningham still lives in the Cunningham Bottoms. Davidson Crossroads is where Bainbridge Road crosses the River Road. Robert Cunningham owned the land at that crossroads; he was the son of old man Cunningham."

Samuel "Sam" Pearsall

On November 16, 1913, Samuel "Sam" Pearsall Jr. and Ophelia Hill were married in Colbert County, Alabama. Sam was born in Sheffield, Alabama, on July 30, 1891.

The parents of Samuel "Sam" Pearsall Jr. were Samuel "Sam" Pearsall Sr. (1860–1918) and Henrietta Fitzgerald Pearsall (1862–1923). Sam Jr. was born into a Black slave family owned by a White cotton planter by the name of Edward Pearsall. According to the 1850 Franklin (Colbert) County, Alabama, Census, Edward Pearsall owned 62 Black slaves.

The siblings of Samuel "Sam" Pearsall Jr. were Jackson Pearsall, Albert Pearsall (1894–1976), Janet Pearsall, Lydia Pearsall, Sylvia Pearsall, Hettie Pearsall Wattson (1900–1985), Mary Pearsall Burt (1899–1985), Louise Pearsall, and Lydia Pearsall.

Sam and Ophelia

For her entire life, Ophelia was born, raised, lived, and died in the Hawkins Creek Community in Colbert County, Alabama. In 1938, Ophelia and Sam built a new house in the community, and they moved into their house located on the same place where Ophelia was born.

Sam and Ophelia lived together for 54 years and two months prior to his death. On February 4, 1968, Sam died at age 76 in the Muscle Shoals area of Alabama.

On Wednesday, February 7, 1968, in the Times Tri-Cities Daily, Florence, Alabama, the following obituary was published. "Sam Pearsall, Jr., Muscle Shoals, 76, life-long resident of Muscle Shoals City, died Monday after a brief illness. He was a member of Mt. Olive Baptist Church, Muscle Shoals. Services will be from Mt. Olive Baptist Church, Wilson Dam Road, Thursday at 2 p.m., Rev. Billy Buford officiating. Burial will be in Pearsall Cemetery, Thompson and Son directing. Surviving are the widow, Mrs. Ophelia Pearsall, Muscle Shoals; a son, Willie Jones, Flint, Michigan; three sisters, Mrs. Hettie Watts, Mrs. Mary Burt, both of Muscle Shoals; Mrs. Louise Pearsall, Buffalo, New York; two brothers, Albert and Jackson, both of Muscle Shoals. He was the son of Sam Pearsall, Sr., and Henrieta Fitzgerald."

On January 19, 1988, Ophelia Hill Pearsall died at Muscle Shoals in Colbert County, Alabama. Ophelia was about six months over the age of 93; she was buried in the Pearsall Cemetery. Note: A grave marker for Ophelia was not found; therefore, she probably does not have a tombstone.

Pruitt, Edna Lee Vinson Kelley

Huston Cobb Jr. interviewed Edna Lee Vinson Pruitt. She was born on November 21, 1902, in Leighton in Colbert County, Alabama.

The mother of Edna Lee Vinson was Margaret Kay Vinson, who was born about 1882. The parents of Margaret were Richard Vinson Sr. and Lizzie Vinson. The siblings of Margaret were Richard Vinson Jr., Vie Vinson, Percy Vinson, Lula M. Vinson, Mozella Vinson, and Alex Vinson. The family was listed as Mulatto.

Percy Vinson was a brother of Margaret Kay Vinson. Percy was born on March 23, 1893, and he served with the United States Army in World War I. Percy died on February 5, 1976, and he was buried in the King Cemetery in Colbert County, Alabama.

The father of Edna Lee Vinson was Benjamin "Ben" Vinson, who was born about 1880. The parents of Ben were Henry Vinson Sr., who was born about 1840 in Virginia, and Tiller "Tilla" Vinson, who was born about 1856 in North Carolina. She was listed as Mulatto in the census records. The siblings of Ben were Henry Vinson, Emmet Vinson, Mary Vinson, Martha Vinson, Horace Vinson, and Edward Vinson.

The 1910 Colbert County, Alabama, Census, Leighton, Precinct 11, Household 54 had the following information: Margaret Vinson, born 1882, Female, Mulatto, 28, Farm Laborer; Benjamin Vinson, Spouse, Male, Black, 30, Farmer; and Edna L. Vinson, Daughter, Female, Mulatto, seven.

Edna said, "My mother and father separated when I was very young; I would go to my Aunt Betsy and go to school. I would spend the summers with my daddy, Ben Vinson. Sometimes I would spend some time in the summer at New Home with my mother's sister, Burgie Pruitt."

Mount New Home Community was on the Cotton Town Road south of Leighton and east of the County Line Road in Colbert County, Alabama. The community was located in the Town Creek Triangle not far northeast of White Oak on Highway 157.

According to the 1920 Colbert County, Alabama, Census, Leighton, Precinct 11, Household 255, Margaret Vinson was a 37-year-old Mulatto female widow who was head of the household and a farm laborer. Edna L. Vinson was listed as a 16-year-old (18) Mulatto female daughter. She was the only child of Margaret and Benjamin Vinson.

Edna said, "My mother later married Emmitt Wallace. His son was like my big brother."

Edna continued, "I picked cotton and cleaned house for fifty cents per day. I went to Galilee Baptist Church. I helped raise money to build the Leighton school. We would sell plates and things, and we had a show to raise money."

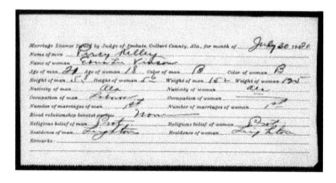

On July 30, 1920, Edna Lee Vinson married Percy Kelley in Colbert County, Alabama. Edna was 18 and Percy was 21 at the time of their marriage.

Edna said, "I was married twice, but this is my last husband. I married Clem Hood, and we moved from here to Chattanooga in the 1930s. He had three sisters and two brothers: Johnny Pruitt in Sheffield, Alabama; Frankie Sheppard of Chattanooga; Louie Pruitt of Akron, Ohio; and Annie Lee Pruitt of Akron, Ohio."

The Black family name Pruitt probably came from the White cotton planters by the name of Pruitt (Preuit). According to the 1860 Lawrence (Colbert) County census, W. Richard Preuit (Pruitt) of "Preuit Oaks Plantation" in Leighton owned 163 Black slaves. Richard was one of the most successful cotton planters in the Town Creek Triangle.

Eventually, Edna moved back to her old home place in Leighton, Alabama. On March 22, 1999, Edna Lee Vinson Kelley Pruitt of Leighton in Colbert County, Alabama, died at 96 years old.

Stanley, Dollie Mae Cobb

About 1985, Huston Cobb Jr. interviewed Dollie Mae Cobb Stanley, who was 82 years old at the time. Dollie was the daughter of Jessee Cobb and Marley Cobb.

The father of Jessee Cobb was Yampe Cobb. According to the 1870 Colbert County, Alabama, Census, all of the family of Yampe Cobb was born in Alabama. In the 1880 census records, Yampe Cobb was listed as Armistead Cobb

The 1870 census record included the following details: 32/32, Yampe Cobb, 31, male, Black, farm laborer; Margaret, 23, female, Black, keeping house; Harriet, 13, female, Black; Tilla, 12, female, Black; Celia, 10, female, Black; Duke, seven, male, Black; Jessee, three, male, Black; Stewart, one, male, Black. In 1880, Harriet Wallace was listed as a stepdaughter. Yampe had other younger children by the name of Victoria and Mandy.

Jessee and Marley Cobb had three sons and three daughters: Obie Cobb, who was in World War II; Wille Cobb, who married Mattie; Harry Cobb; Cora Cobb; Dollie Cobb; and Effie Cobb.

Dollie was raised in the Town Creek Triangle near the edge of the Tennessee River. She first attended a little school near Bethel Colbert Church. Ms. Lena Miller taught at Bethel. Later, Dollie attended school at Mt. Pleasant. After leaving Mt. Pleasant, Dollie went to Courtland to a boarding school; it caught fire.

Dollie Cobb Stanley married in 1924. After marriage, she and her husband moved from the area of Bethel Colbert to Sheffield.

The Black members of the Stanley family probably got their name from their ancestors who were former slaves of White plantation owners. According to census records, those Whites slave owners included Andrew Stanley, Edward Stanley, Ellen Stanley, James Stanley, and Nathaniel Stanley.

Stanley, Reverend O. C.

About 1985, Huston Cobb Jr. interviewed Reverend O. C. "Ocie" Stanley Sr., who was born on May 4, 1904. O. C. Stanley was the son of Henry Stanley and Mary Whiteside Stanley; Mary was born about 1875.

The parents of Mary were Fred Whiteside and Rosa Whiteside. Fred and Rosa Whiteside were probably born as slaves in present-day Colbert County, Alabama. Fred was born about 1852, and Rosa was born about 1851.

According to the 1920 Colbert County, Alabama, Census, Fred and Rosa Whiteside had two Mulatto grandsons, who were Simpson Pride and Mose Pride, living in their household. In addition, the 1930 Colbert County, Alabama, Census listed Ross Stanley as 27 years old and living with his brother O. C. Stanley at Brick Community.

Reverend O. C. Stanley Sr. married Elsie Lee King Stanley. They were married about 1923, probably in Colbert County, Alabama. The Black family with the surname King most likely descended from the White slave owners of the King Family, who settled much of the Town Creek Triangle.

In the 1940 Colbert County, Alabama, Census, Brick Community, Household Number 217, O. C. Stanley was a married 35-year-old Black male farm owner with a fifth-grade education living east of the County Line or Leighton Road. Also in his household were the following individuals: his wife, Elsie Lee King Stanley, who was 33 years old; Annie Liza Stanley, who was 16 years old; Hattie Lou Stanley, who was 13 years old; Naomia L. Stanley, who was 11 years old; Henry Leon Stanley, who was nine years old; Helen Mary Stanley, who was seven years old; Louis Anna Stanley, who was five years old; Thornton S. Stanley, who was three years old; and Pric Stanley, who was seven months old. Three additional children of the Stanley family were O. C. Stanley Jr., Sara Stanley Neil, and Manervia Stanley.

Hattie Lou Stanley, daughter of O. C. and Elsie Stanley, married Fred King. After Fred and Hattie separated, she married Willie Booker.

On August 4, 1987, Reverend O. C. "Ocie" Stanley

Sr. died in Colbert County, Alabama. Basically, he lived his entire life in the Town Creek Triangle. O. C. Stanley was buried at Bethel Colbert MB Church Cemetery in Colbert County, Alabama (Find A Grave Memorial Number 130560357).

Henry Leon Stanley

On May 3, 1930, O. C. and Elsie Stanley had a son, Henry Leon Stanley, who was born in Colbert County, Alabama. On May 31, 1947, Henry married Mattie Eva Bates Wilkerson in Colbert County, Alabama. Mattie was the daughter of Green Bates and Gazell Johnson.

On September 6, 1952, Henry Leon Stanley married a second time to Helen Louise Gadd in Colbert County, Alabama. Dr. Wayne Stanley of Colbert County is the son of Henry Leon Stanley and Helen Louise Gadd Stanley.

Henry L. Stanley and Helen Gadd

Helen was born on May 14, 1926, in Tuscumbia in Colbert County, Alabama, to King (Cane) H. Gadd and Ruth Pride. On November 15, 1992, Helen Louise Gadd Stanley died in Colbert County, Alabama, and she was buried in the Bethel Colbert MB Church Cemetery (Find A Grave Memorial Number 130546162).

Henry Leon Stanley married a third time to Helen Jarman. She was probably descended from the slaves of a White slave owner known as Amos Jarman.

On March 29, 2011, Henry Leon Stanley died at 80 years old in Florence in Lauderdale County, Alabama. He was buried in the Bethel Colbert MB Church Cemetery in Colbert County, Alabama (Find A Grave Memorial Number 130544767).

Helen Mary Stanley Cobb

On May 3, 1930, O. C. and Elsie Stanley had a daughter by the name of Helen Mary Stanley. She was born in Colbert County, Alabama. Helen married Ernest Cobb (1929–2000), the brother of Huston Cobb Jr.

On October 7, 2019, Helen Mary Stanley Cobb died at age 87 in Rocky River in Cuyahoga County, Ohio. She was buried by her husband in the Houston Cobb Sr. Family cemetery in Colbert County, Alabama (Find A Grave Memorial Number 28762442).

Helen Stanley and Ernest Cobb

Andrew Watkins

On September 7, 1985, Huston Cobb Jr. interviewed Andrew Watkins, who was 92 years old; Andrew was born on May 15, 1893. At the time he was interviewed by Mr. Cobb, Andrew was mentally sharp as a tack. Andrew said, "My full name is Andrew Elmore Curtis Watkins."

The Watkins name of this Black family probably came from the White slave owner by the name of R. S. Watkins. According to the 1860 Franklin (Colbert) County, Alabama, Census, R. S. Watkins owned 17 Black slaves.

The parents of Andrew Watkins were Giles W. Watkins (1856–1938) and Harriett Alice Watkins (1862–1937). Andrew had three brothers and five sisters. His brothers were Robert G. Watkins (2/20/1885–12/21/1978), Eddie F. Watkins (9/2/1886–1/16/1979), and William Watkins. His sisters were Margaret Watkins Goodloe (5/15/1888–12/29/1974); Lucindy Watkins Leigh; Martha Watkins Thompson (6/14/1895–12/19/1998), who married Percy Thompson (1894–1993); Mary L. Watkins Goodloe (4/28/1898–2/21/1953); and Addie Watkins Phillips.

White Family of Barton

Andrew Watkins and his family were descendants of the Black slaves of the Barton Family in the area of Cherokee in the western portion of present-day Colbert County, Alabama. The Barton folks were a White family who owned cotton plantations and Black slaves.

The Community of Barton was named in honor of the family of Dr. Hugh Barton. Hugh was the son of Roger and Margaret Barton of Frederick County, Virginia. Hugh and Mary (Polly) Magdalene Shirley Barton moved from Greene County, Tennessee, to Franklin (Colbert) County, Alabama; they had 11 children. Hugh died on February 19, 1853, and Polly died on December 27, 1852; both died in present-day Colbert County, and they were buried in the Rutland Cemetery in Cherokee, Alabama.

The oldest child of Hugh and Polly Barton was Armistead Barton, who built Barton Hall Plantation Mansion on the Natchez Trace near Buzzard Roost in Colbert County, Alabama. From 1836 through 1844, Armistead Barton entered some 8,400 acres of land in Franklin (Colbert) County.

Barton Hall Plantation Mansion

Armistead Barton, the older brother of Arthur C. Barton, was one of the wealthiest cotton planters near Cherokee in Colbert County, Alabama. In 1850, Amanda C. Cook Barton, the wife of the late Armistead Barton, owned 155 Black slaves.

Arthur Crozier Barton

Arthur Crozier Barton was the fourth child of Hugh and Polly Barton. Arthur became a very wealthy White cotton planter who owned a big plantation just east of Cherokee, Alabama. Arthur was born in 1806 and he died about 1892.

According to the 1860 census of old Franklin (Colbert) County, Arthur C. Barton owned 72 Black slaves. Between October 1838 and March 1851, Arthur entered some 1,600 acres of land, most of which was in Township 4 South and Range 13 West around present-day Barton in Colbert County, Alabama.

The grandparents of Andrew Watkins were some of the Black slaves of Arthur C. Barton. Andrew Watkins stated, "Arthur owned my grandparents; we found the receipt where he bought them. Arthur Barton bought my grandfather and two other Black male slaves in North Carolina for $800.00. One of the men was named Adam, my granddaddy; he did not have a surname. The other two men were John and Pete. Pete was my granddaddy's daddy, and John was granddaddy's first cousin."

Andrew continued, "Old man Barton owned my grandmother, too, before she married my granddaddy; she came from Richmond, Virginia. I heard her say that they sold her on the block, and they said she was 19, but her mother said she was 16 years old; she was just large for her age. Arthur worked my grandparents on his cotton plantation. My mother, Harriett Alice Watkins, was born in 1863 to my grandparents, who were the slaves of Arthur Barton; she was just a baby when the Civil War ended in 1865.

"Old man Barton done something that other slave owners did not do; he had a colored woman as his wife. Her name was on all the deeds—Jane Barton and Arthur Barton; my deed has both of their names. Arthur and Aunt Jane have tombstones.

"Arthur had his house, and he built Aunt Jane a house with about enough room to drive a car between the two. They did not have concrete then; he had a brick walk connecting his house and the house of Aunt Jane. All old man Barton had to do was come out of his house and go right over to Aunt Jane's house.

"Arthur Barton had two daughters by his colored wife, Aunt Jane, and each one of the daughters got 600 acres which were joined together. I bought my land from Ms. Josephine Barton, one of his daughters. Ms. Josephine weighed about 300 pounds; she was a great big woman. She always called me her boy.

"From what I understand, Arthur paid another White girl to be a buddy to his daughter Josephine. Josephine could play a piano; old man Barton had a piano, and he would have people come to his home, and Josephine would play the piano for them."

Andrew Watkins Folks

"After the Civil War, my granddaddy bought the old Methodist Church up here and two acres of land for three hundred dollars; it was originally a White church. The White folks had a little corner for their carriage driver to set. The church was plastered over head, and the walls were plastered."

Andrew said, "This land of mine is the same land of the cotton plantation that Arthur Barton owned. Arthur gave my grandmother a lifetime home, and he gave Aunt Kate Walker a lifetime home right down here at Barton. We lived on one side of the road and Aunt Kate lived on the other side; we moved from there when I was about four years old."

Andrew Watkins served in the United States Army during World War I for 18 months. He was first assigned to Camp Dodge, Iowa. Camp Dodge was constructed in 1917 and was the training camp of the 88th Division known as the "Fighting Blue Devils." Andrew left Camp Dodge after training and went straight to France. Andrew was in France for nine months, and he said, "When the war was over, I was on the front lines in France."

Andrew Watkins married Callie Watkins, who was born on April 9, 1895. Callie died on November 25, 1979, at age 84. She was buried at Zion Number 1 Missionary Baptist Church Cemetery in Colbert County, Alabama (Find A Grave Memorial Number 39122722).

Andrew Watkins lived and died on the cotton plantation where his grandparents worked as Black slaves of Arthur Barton. The family of Andrew was fortunate that Arthur Barton became part of his extended family, and he gave Andrew's grandmother a home on the old plantation.

At the conclusion of his interview, Huston Cobb Jr. made the following statements, "Mr. Andrew Watkins took us to an old graveyard where no one had been buried for approximately 50 years. Some of my wife's great-grand-people were buried there; we took pictures of the tombstones. We had a hard time finding the graveyard because it had grown up so bad; no one knew where it was except Mr. Watkins. It was an experience of a lifetime to go back and fine those old tombstones; some of them were handmade as I had never seen before. The writing was gone off those that were handmade, and some of the others were legible."

Death of Andrew Watkins

On June 23, 1993, Mr. Andrew Watkins died in Colbert County, Alabama, at the ripe old age of 100. He was buried in the Zion Number 1 Missionary Baptist Church Cemetery near Cherokee in Colbert County, Alabama (Find A Grave Memorial Number 18770590).

Conclusion

I really appreciate the foresight of Mr. Huston Cobb Jr. for interviewing his elders during the 1980s. He saved a treasure trove of information that would have been lost forever had he not took his time to visit them and record their history.

I also learned so much from Mr. Cobb, and from the writing and researching for the completion of this book about Black folks who called the Town Creek Triangle and the Muscle Shoals area home. I am so grateful and honored that I was lucky enough to meet an elder with so much information and knowledge that we could coauthor a book together.

Huston Cobb Jr., former UNA Trustee, with Senator Mitch McConnell and Elaine Chao

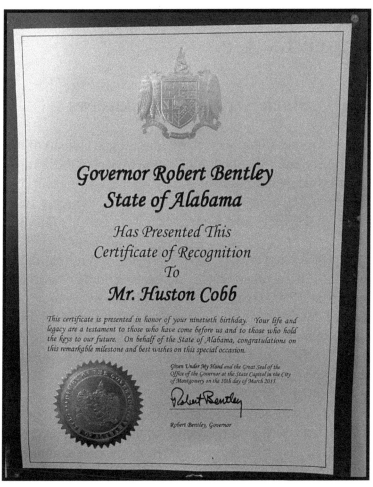

Governor *Robert Bentley*
State of Alabama

Has Presented This
Certificate of Recognition
To

Mr. Huston Cobb

This certificate is presented in honor of your ninetieth birthday. Your life and legacy are a testament to those who have come before us and to those who hold the keys to our future. On behalf of the State of Alabama, congratulations on this remarkable milestone and best wishes on this special occasion.

Given Under My Hand and the Great Seal of the Office of the Governor at the State Capitol in the City of Montgomery on the 10th day of March 2015.

Robert Bentley, Governor

Certificate of Recognition presented to Huston Cobb Jr. by former Alabama Governor Robert Bentley on his ninetieth birthday

Appendix A

Black Slaves of Chickasaws

Around 1740, Scotsman James Logan Colbert of the Carolinas came with Scots Irish Indian traders of the British/ English merchants into Chickasaw country of present-day northwest Alabama. Colbert settled near the mouth of Bear Creek on the Tennessee River, where he raised his family.

In a letter to Governor Harrison of Virginia dated July 25, 1783, Colbert stated, "I was born in the Carolinas, and about 1740, (I) moved to the Chickasaw Nation and married into the tribe." Colbert married three Chickasaw women who bore him at least nine children: William, Sally (Love), Celia (McLish), George, Levi, Samuel, Joseph, James, and Susan (Allen).

Captain James Logan Colbert (title given by the British) led Chickasaw raids on French and Spanish vessels navigating the Mississippi River, thereby accumulating over 150 Black slaves prior to his death. From the 1775 start of the Chickamauga War and until his death, James Logan Colbert and his half-blood Chickasaw sons were allied with Lower Cherokee Chief Doublehead and Creek Chief Alexander McGillivary, who were fighting the encroachment of White settlers on their ancestral lands. The three tribes were being supplied arms and ammunition by the British and were fighting to protect their homelands and hunting grounds in northwest Alabama.

On July 5, 1782, a declaration was made by Spanish merchant Silbestre Labadie, who had been a captive of James Logan Colbert in the spring of 1782 when his boat, slaves, and goods were captured at Chickasaw Bluff on the Mississippi River. Labadie stated that James Logan Colbert, "was about 60 years old, possessed of good health, and a strong constitution. An active man, despite his years, he had a violent temper, and was capable of enduring the greatest hardship. He had lived among the Chickasaws for 40 years and boasted that he was owner of a fine house and some hundred and fifty Blacks. He said he had several sons by Chickasaw women, who were very important chiefs in that nation."

On January 7, 1784, while returning toward home after visiting with Creek Chief Alexander McGillivary, his friend and brother-in-law to his son William, James Logan Colbert was killed by his Black slave Cesar or from being thrown from his horse. After his death, the Black slaves of James Logan Colbert were divided and given to his children. Some of his children sold their slaves, and some of those Black folks remained in northwest Alabama.

George Colbert and his brother Levi Colbert, sons of James Logan Colbert, became very famous cotton planters with large plantations. They were also owners of numerous Black slaves in present-day Colbert County, Alabama.

Chickasaw Chief Levi Colbert

Levi Colbert was born about 1759, and he became a Chief of the Chickasaw Nation. Levi was a successful plantation owner, cotton planter, and owner of Black slaves inherited from his father. For several years, Levi lived on the Natchez Trace at Buzzard Roost Spring, about seven miles southwest of the ferry of his brother George Colbert, in present-day Colbert County, Alabama.

Levi had a fine house at Buzzard Roost on the Natchez Trace that he gave to his daughter, Phalishta "Pat" Malacha Colbert, and her husband, Kilpatrick Carter. According to the 1830 Colbert County slave census records, Pat and Kilpatrick Carter owned 45 Black slaves. They were large landowners with four 640-acre sections of land adjacent to the Natchez Trace near Buzzard Roost Spring in present-day Colbert County, Alabama.

Martha "Patsey" Colbert, another daughter of Levi, was born in 1820; she married Jackson Kemp. According to the Colbert County land records, Martha and Jackson Kemp owned nearly three sections of land in the county.

On June 2, 1834, Levi Colbert died at the home of his daughter at her Buzzard Roost Spring home in Colbert County, Alabama. He was 74 years of age at his death, and he lies in an unknown burial site. It was speculated that Levi Colbert was buried near his original Buzzard Roost home in Colbert County.

Chickasaw Chief George

George Colbert was born about 1744, and he became a Chief of the Chickasaw Nation; he married two daughters of Doublehead—Tuskiahooto and Saleechie. From 1798 until 1819, George operated a ferry crossing of the Natchez Trace on the Tennessee River.

In addition to operating a ferry crossing, George was a cotton planter with many Black slaves that he inherited from his father, James Logan Colbert. According to Colbert County land records, George Colbert was an owner of a cotton plantation with some 2,560 acres of land in the county.

Home of George Colbert

The home of George Colbert was the first government house built specifically for the Chickasaw chief in the Colbert County area of which we have any records. His home was built between 1801 and 1806 just south of his ferry at the Tennessee River crossing of the Natchez Trace. In a portion of the Chickasaw Treaty of December 1801, General James Wilkinson of the United States Army agreed to build a large dwelling house for George and his family, cabins for travelers, a store, stables, a new ferry boat, and other facilities for George to operate the ferry crossing for the general public.

The government home of George Colbert was the

kind of house that a well-to-do frontiersman would have built. His home was a frame house, whereas most of the first White settler homes were made of logs with large rooms and a hall between the two rooms called a dog trot.

At his home in Colbert County, George had more than a dozen log cabins for the families of his Black slaves. The walls of the slave cabins were said to be made of four 30-inch-wide poplar logs.

George owned and ran his ferry where the Natchez Trace crossed the Tennessee River from present-day Lauderdale County to present-day Colbert County, Alabama. It was said that the ferry of George Colbert transported the army of Andrew Jackson across the Tennessee River in 1815. For the crossing, George Colbert charged Jackson a sum of $75,000.00, quite a bit of money for that time. George reportedly gave the high charges because building improvements at his ferry were not completed as agreed upon with General James Wilkinson.

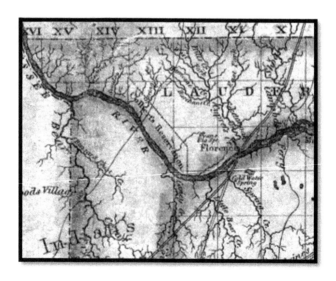

On September 20, 1816, George Colbert became the owner of 16 square miles in Colbert's Reserve in present-day Lauderdale County, Alabama. His reserve on the north side of the Tennessee River was nearly centered on his ferry crossing. On May 15, 1819, George deeded his reserve back to the United States.

Until about 1819, George lived in present-day Colbert County, Alabama, at the Colbert's Ferry crossing of the Tennessee River on the Natchez Trace. After the death of his Cherokee wife, Tuskiahooto, in 1818, George moved with his other Cherokee wife, Saleechie, to his plantation in Tupelo, Mississippi, which was the capital of the Chickasaw Nation.

Colbert Lands

Even though he had a large plantation near Tupelo, George Colbert and some of his children owned large tracts of land and Black slaves in present-day Colbert County. At his two plantations, George worked some 140 Black slaves and became one of the wealthiest of the Colbert siblings.

The Treaty with the Chickasaws on May 24, 1834, allowed individual Chickasaw Indian people to own their reservations or tracts of land they lived upon and improved in Colbert County, Alabama. George Colbert owned all the land in Sections 1, 2, 11, and 12 of Township 3 South and Range 14 West in Colbert County, Alabama.

Other Chickasaw citizens, including children and grandchildren of James Logan Colbert, also owned land in Colbert County and had Black slaves. Pamela Colbert Reynolds, a daughter of George Colbert and the wife of

Francis Reynolds, son of Indian agent Benjamin Reynolds, entered land in six sections in Townships 2, 3, 4 South and Ranges 13 and 15 West. Pamela owned three 640-acre sections of land in present-day Colbert County. According to the 1840 census records of present-day Colbert County, Pamela Colbert and her husband, Francis Reynolds, owned 33 Black slaves.

Removal and Death

By the time he was removed west on November 14, 1837, Chickasaw Chief George Colbert owned some 150 Black slaves. His slaves farmed his property holdings in present-day Colbert County, Alabama, and Mississippi.

Chickasaw Chief George Colbert died on November 7, 1839, in Indian Territory west of the Mississippi River. He was buried near Fort Towson, and he was said to be ninety-five years old.

Black Slaves of Cherokees

Doublehead was a Lower Cherokee Chief of the Chickamauga Confederacy in the Muscle Shoals area, and he was also the owner of some 40 Black slaves. Ocuma, the sister of Doublehead, and her husband, John Melton, owned some 60 Black slaves. The slaves of the Melton Family were purchased by General Andrew Jackson and remained in North Alabama.

In the Cotton Gin Treaty of January 7, 1806, Doublehead had a cotton gin placed near the home of John and Ocuma Melton at Melton's Bluff on the Elk River Shoals in present-day Lawrence County, Alabama. On November

22, 1816, David Melton, son of John and Ocuma, of the Cherokee Nation sold the land and slaves at Melton's Bluff to General Andrew Jackson. The slaves of Andrew Jackson worked the cotton fields of old Melton along the eastern Shoals. Jackson sold the property in 1827 when he was running for President of the United States.

Cuttyatoy

During the Chickamauga War on May 9, 1788, a small group of Black slaves were taken captive by a Lower Cherokee Chief by the name of Cuttyatoy and his Creek and Cherokee warriors. The slaves belonged to the John Brown family; John was killed, and his family members and Black slaves were captured near the Lower Chickamauga Cherokee town of Nickajack on the southeast edge of Tennessee.

John Brown and his family were floating down the Tennessee River near the present-day state lines of Georgia, Tennessee, and Alabama when the incident occurred. Members of the Brown Family taken prisoner included Jane Brown, the wife of John, two of her sons, George and Joseph, and two of her daughters.

Chief Cuttyatoy took the Black slaves to his village at the western end of Elk River Shoals of the Tennessee River in present-day Lawrence County, Alabama. The Lower Cherokee village of Cuttyatoy was on Gilchrist Island, across the river from the mouth of Elk River. The home of Cuttyatoy was located on an island on the south side of the Tennessee River near the mouth of Spring Creek.

In time, Joseph Brown, son of John and Jane Brown,

escaped from Cherokee captivity and joined the army of Tennessee volunteers commanded by General Andrew Jackson. Joseph became a colonel during the Creek Indian War. During the Battle of Talladega on November 9, 1813, Colonel Joseph Brown learned from mixed-blood Charles Butler where the Black slaves of the Brown family were being held by Cuttyatoy.

According to the *American Whig Review*, Volume 15, Issue 87, March 1852, page 247, "Colonel (Joseph) Brown…a participant in the battle of Talledega (November 9, 1813)…met Charles Butler… and learned from him that…Chief Cuttyatoy, was still alive…he was then living on an island in the Tennessee River, near the mouth of Elk River, and that he had with him several…taken by him at Nickajack on the 9th of May, 1788…with ten picked men, Brown proceeded to the island, went to the head man's (Cuttyatoy) lodge and exhibited to him General (Andrew) Jackson's order, and demanded that Cuttyatoy's (slaves) be immediately sent over to Fort Hampton (in present-day Limestone County)…In crossing the river, Colonel Brown and his men took up the (slaves), and Cuttyatoy's wife behind them, to carry them over the water while the Indian men crossed on a raft (Brown's Ferry) higher up (stream). Colonel Joseph Brown and his men reached Fort Hampton that morning while Cuttyatoy and his men arrived in the afternoon."

Joseph Brown was born on August 2, 1772, and he was 15 years old at the time he was taken captive by the Chickamauga Faction of Lower Cherokees. Joseph Brown became a preacher prior to retaking his father's Black slaves. He settled in the Community of Bodenham just three miles west of Pulaski, Tennessee.

On February 4, 1868, Reverend Joseph Brown died after being burned by falling into his fireplace. He was buried in the Mt. Moriah Cemetery some two miles west of Pulaski, Tennessee.

Duwali—Bowle

Lower Cherokee Chief Bowle (Duwali), born circa 1756, was a fierce half-blood son of a Scots father and Cherokee mother. While fighting with Doublehead during the Chickamauga War, Duwali was leader of a band of Lower Cherokees who killed 13 White people of William and Alexander Scott's party from Williamsburg, South Carolina.

During the assault on the Scott flotilla at the Muscle Shoals, Chief Bowle and his warriors captured 21 Black slaves. It is thought that some of the Black slaves that Duwali took captive were part of the 60 slaves sold to General Andrew Jackson when he purchased Melton's Bluff in November 1816.

In 1794, members of the Scott party were trying to reach the Natchez District when they were attacked near the Elk River Shoals of the Tennessee River at Melton's Bluff in Lawrence County, Alabama. Duwali's warriors killed all Whites in the party except for some women and children who were set adrift on the Shoals. Since there was no mention of the slaves when Duwali moved west, Doublehead and John Melton probably took the Black slaves for their cotton plantation and farming operations.

This act of piracy at the Muscle Shoals of the Tennessee River in northwest Alabama received so much publicity that Bowle was forced to flee to the Arkansas country. Later, Chief Bowle settled with his band on the Neches River and the Sabine River in Texas.

Some say that Duwali left the Muscle Shoals shortly after 1794. However, according to United States Agent to the Cherokees Return J. Meigs' letter of January 22, 1810, to United States Secretary of War, Chief Bowle's passport for 63 Cherokees moving west of the Mississippi was issued to him on January 10, 1810. The 83-year-old Duwali died on the battlefield fighting the Texans on July 16, 1839.

Captain John D. Chisholm

Captain John D. Chisholm acted as an attorney for Chickamauga Cherokee Chief Doublehead. After the death of Doublehead, John Chisholm and Nance, sister of Doublehead, had a disagreement over Black slaves. Chisholm claimed the slaves belonged to him, while Nance was saying that three of the slaves belonged to her.

John D. Chisholm accompanied Tahluntuskee and the Lower Cherokees west. Even though he was a White man, Chisholm represented the Old Settlers in Washington, D. C.

In January 1818, Chisholm returned to Lauderdale County and settled some five miles north of Florence, Alabama. He entered some 1,200 acres and worked his cotton plantation with his Black slaves. John Chisholm died in 1828 and was buried in the Chisholm Cemetery on the west side of the Chisholm Road.

Appendix B

The following pages contain letters sent from and to Mr. Huston Cobb Jr. that he has collected over the years.

The first three letters are examples of the correspondence between Huston and Sadie Long while he was in the U.S. Navy; the first contains the "be as one" phrase that troubled Sadie, as described on page 93.

The fourth and final letter was sent to Huston from his mother, Nazareth.

From Sadie to Huston
September 18, 1945

Rout 1 Box 32 le
Sheffield, Ala,
Sept. 18, 1945

Dearest Huston,

Your letter was mine yesterday and it was indeed a thrill to hear from you, I am feeling fine hoping you are okey.

I am answering your letter right back because I've planned to go down South near Georgia to teach in my cousin's place for a while and I guess I'll go about the 5th of Oct. and I would like to hear from you again before I leave if possible, then I'll write you again after changing address.

Now Huston for getting down to brass tacks as you said. Sure we can be as one it only depends on what you want to make of anything. And I do care for you. Now is that plain English? "Smile"

I don't know how I am
going to like down there but
I guess I could put up with
for a while any way and
hearing from home and you
too maybe I won't get so
lonesome.

I'll have to close now I'm
in a hurry So we are depending
on each other.

As Ever Yours
Leslie

From Sadie to Huston
October 18, 1945

Route 1 Box 4
Pitaview, Ala.
Oct. 18, 1945

Dearest Huston,

I recieved your letter only and you can bet your life I was glad to hear from you after so long a time, though it found me well and going to school everyday but I'll have you to understand that I gets plenty lonesome.

I have your picture here with me, Huston (believe it or not) The one you sent a long time ago it is very much like you. You say you enjoy lookin at my picture though I knew it wasn't good but it was the only one I had on hand.

And about Frank Hall, no I hadn't heard about him being a father, so I guess he is proud of his little daughter. I suppose I'll see your sister some Frank and Mr. Austin this evening.

Huston, you asked me to tell you all about this place, well, it is just on out the Macy place, a good ways from Ga. and not so far either. The name of the reason where I am is Glenville and I am teaching the 1st through 3rd grade and as small it is a few. These children who live [illegible]

258

II

I don't know how long I am to be down here but I hope I'll be home ~~when~~ when you return, and I hope that some time soon.

Huston, I am not trying to be inquisitive and I hope I am not asking too much, but what I want to know is Mrs Stanley your personal friend? Though if she is it's alright because it ~~doesn't~~ It doesn't ~~concern~~ mean me, I just asked you.

Well we been going to church every Sunday since I've been here but Sun. I was going to stay home and rest because I am tired. — As I've about ~~my~~ (I have two or three)

I will close now, and write soon, so until I hear from you,

"Keep your chin up
until I see you"

Sincerely,
Indie

259

From Huston to Sadie
June 19, 1947

R.1. Box 121
Leighton, Ala.
June 19, 1947

Dearest Sadie

Hello Sweet. How
are you feeling today?

Well for my part I
am feeling fine, only
you stay on my mind
a little to much for
comfort.

I received your note
Tuesday and that was
sooner than I expected
but that note went
just as good as a
letter, all that matters

is that it's from you.
You got there in plenty
time. Was Mose lying
about Mase was going
to take you up there
in his car?

Tell your room mate I
say hello. There isn't
much to say this time
I guess you can see
that. but you tell me
a lot when you write.
I guess this is all
for now. yours
Gotha

From Nazareth to Huston
December 31, 1945

Leighton ala R1. Box 66
Dec 31-1945

Huston Jr.

Dear Son how are you by this time
fine I hope this leaves all well
we got your letter saturday and
was glad to hear from you and to
know that you are still doing fine
you say you alls mail goes by ship
now I thought something we
would be longer hearing from
you now then we useter. I guess
you have got my letter by now
telling you about the nice gift
you sent us that is so sweet of you
Caroline is here with us for a while
she say its time for you to come home
the last time she was here you were
at home. Ness and her family was here
yesterday sunday. the children are fiping
to go to school they start back on the 3th
Frank Watson was by here last week
he say he had wrote you. it is lots of the
boys comming home now. We are still
looking for you. of course you know
as I do that it takes the government
so long to do any thing. it is slow but
shure. Arnie Lee and all is well and
say hello to you. so I guess this is all for today
from your mother nazareth

Index

A

Abernathy, John T. 51, 52
Aldridge, Earl 141
Alexander Plantation 31, 115, 116, 118, 119, 121, 122
Alexander, Jake 116, 121
Alexander, James 116, 122
Alexander, Thomas Jefferson 116, 117, 118, 121
Alexander, William 117, 121
American Missionary Association 181, 182, 183
Ashford, Willie A. 64
Austin's Mill 85

B

Bailey, Bolin 154, 155
Bailey, Haney 155, 156, 157, 158
Bailey, Hirmon "Haney" 155, 154
Bailey, Levi A. 36
Bainbridge Loop 9, 32, 33
Barton 54, 59, 153, 236, 237, 240
Barton, Armistead 237
Barton, Arthur 238, 239, 240
Barton, Arthur C. 237, 238
Barton, Hugh 237, 238
Barton, Josephine 239
Bates, Emma Kate 189
Bates, Lucille 225
Bates, Mattie Eva 234
Bates, Percy 225
Bates, Willie C. 175, 177

C

E

F

G

Gadd, Helen Louise 37, 234, 235
Gholston, Walter 95
Gibson, Sylvanus 139
Graves, Arthur 25, 99, 100, 105, 106, 108, 109, 110, 111, 112
Graves, Frank 106, 108, 112
Green Onion Plantation 52, 72, 73, 75
Gregg Tavern 29
Griffin, Clifton 139
Griffin, G. W. 58, 116
Griffin, Mack 55, 58, 116
Griffin, Mary 58
Griffin, Mattie 115, 116
Griffin, Mattie (Matt) 115, 116
Griffin, Theo 139

H

Hall, Frank 89, 90
Hampton, Angie 197
Hampton, Cora 189, 192, 193
Hampton, George 223
Hampton, Manoah 190
Handy, W. C. 152
Hawkins Creek 33, 153, 191, 226, 227
Hayes, Harry 189, 191
Hayes, Lucinda Jarmon 189, 190, 191, 192
Hennigan, Samuel S. 52
Hodges, Fleming 134, 135
Hodges, John 129, 133, 134, 135
Hodges, Sallie 134
Hog Island 59, 60, 61, 62

I

Ingram, Benjamin 178, 179, 180
Ingram, Fred 189, 193
Irwin, Price 133

J

Jacobs, Billy 131, 132
Jacobs, Tass 136, 142
Jacobs, Willie 136, 137
Jarman Lane 33, 44, 189
Jarman, Amos 33, 42, 43, 44, 52, 56, 81, 190, 235
Jarman, Hall 52
Jarman, Nazarene 44
Jarman, Nazerine 59
Jarmon, Albert J. 189, 190, 192
Jarmon, Arthur 158, 191
Jarmon, Ira 189, 192
Jarmon, John 189, 192, 193
Jarmon, Lillie Bell 189, 192, 193, 194
Jarmon, Lucinda 189, 190, 191, 192
Jeanes, Anna T. 186
Jeffrey's Crossroads 28, 29, 30, 33
Johnson, Cole 47, 48, 194
Johnson, Coleman 194, 196, 222, 223, 224
Johnson, Fannie 24, 71, 72, 77, 78, 79, 207
Johnson, Irena 223
Johnson, Jerry J. 194, 196, 197
Johnson, Jerry J. "Gooden" 194, 195, 196, 197
Johnson, John 9, 44, 63, 72, 75, 222
Johnson, John H. 52, 62, 63, 71, 72, 73, 74, 75, 76
Johnson, Mamie 194, 195, 198, 199
Johnson, Martha 196
Johnson, Martin 62, 72, 76, 77, 78, 194, 209, 222
Johnson, Mattie 168, 193, 196
Johnson, York 222, 223

K

Kattygisky 61, 62, 63, 64
Kelsoe, William Todd 116
King, Claude 29, 30, 67, 69
King, Clyde 29
King, Ella 155
King, Elsie 37, 65, 233
King, Emmitt 69
King, Fred 200, 234
King, Lila Vinson 37, 44, 199, 200, 201, 205, 207
King, Walter James 199, 207, 208
Kittiakaska Creek 62, 63, 64, 65, 66, 72, 73
Kittiakaska Spring 72, 75

L

LaGrange 9, 17, 18, 19, 20, 22, 23, 27, 201, 205
Lawrence, George 108
Layton, Robert 29, 93
Leach, Cain 181
Lee, Mildred Brackin 123
Leigh, William 30, 31
Leighton Training School 31, 86, 87, 88, 153, 283
Little, Ida 167, 168, 169, 170
Little, Sallie Mae 168, 169
Little, Walter 168, 169
Long, Harry 59, 86, 217, 226
Long, Harry Winston 211
Long, Jean 86, 111, 113
Long, Lois 25
Long, Mary 35, 86
Long, Nellie M. 25, 210, 211, 212, 217
Long, Sadie 59, 86, 87, 88, 90, 92, 97, 255, 256, 258, 260
Long, William Mansel 111
Long, Willie 95
Looney, Martha 128

LouAllen, Larry 149
Lowery, Bryant 140, 142
Lowery, P. B. 120, 121, 138, 142

M

R

Roland, Jim 162, 163, 164
Rosenwald 53, 54, 168, 187, 188, 193

S

Saunders, Turner 18
Savage, Rosella 159, 160, 162, 163, 164, 167
Savage, Tom 159, 160, 162, 163, 177
Shaw Cemetery 50
Shaw Road 46, 49, 50, 92
Shaw, Baldy 46, 49, 50
Shegog Creek 44
Sherrod, Benjamin 14, 15
Shoal Town 9, 61
Sledge, Abe 21, 26
Sledge, Emma 26
Sledge, Percy 27
Smith, Bessie 150, 151, 152
Smith, Georgia 174
Smith, William 150
Spangler, George Granville 155, 156, 217
Stanley, Alex 47
Stanley, Andrew 39, 232
Stanley, Dollie Cobb 232
Stanley, Edward 39, 232
Stanley, Elsie 37, 65, 234, 235
Stanley, Hattie Lou 233
Stanley, Helen 37, 235
Stanley, Henry Leon 37, 233, 234, 235
Stanley, O. C. 37, 232, 233, 234
Stanley, Wayne 37, 38, 234
Stover, John 129, 130
Stover, Johnny 139

T

U

V

Vinson, Henry 229
Vinson, Lizzie 228
Vinson, Lula Mae 189, 192, 228
Vinson, Margaret 229, 230
Vinson, Percy 228, 229
Vinson, Richard 228

W

Walker, Kate 240
Washington, Booker T. 53, 186
Watkins, Andrew 236, 238, 239, 240, 241
Watkins, Robert G. 236
Westside 24, 30, 49
Whiteside, Fred 173, 175, 232
Whiteside, Phil 194, 221
Wilburn, Arthur 141
Wilburn, Cadle 138, 143, 145
Williams, Emma 145, 146
Willis, Will 132

Y

Young, Reason 147

About the Author: Huston Cobb Jr.

Huston Cobb Jr., a descendant of Black slaves, was born at his family's small frame house on March 10, 1925, in the Town Creek Triangle of Colbert County, Alabama, where he spent the vast majority of his life. He was reared in a Christian home and was educated in the segregated Black schools. Huston and his family survived the Great Depression with relative ease because of their hard work ethic and successful agricultural activities.

Prior to graduating at Leighton Training School in 1944, Huston was drafted and served as naval stevedore in the United States Navy at Pearl Harbor in Hawaii while his fellow classmates were receiving their diplomas. Huston was discharged in April 1946, and he arrived home exactly two years from the day he left. Upon his arrival home after serving his country, segregation requirements forced him to use public facilities separate from the White folks.

After the Civil Rights Act of the 1960s, Huston, a foreman with the Tennessee Valley Authority, finally got the right to use the same facilities as the Whites. Huston said, "For once, I lived like a White man with my family going on bus tours and seeing much of our country because I could afford a vacation."

Huston became a political advocate and joined the Republican Party. He ran on the same platform for state representative as Republican Governor Guy Hunt. Huston was politically active and his support was highly sought by local, state, and national political figures from both the Democrat and Republican parties. From all candidates running for national offices such as president, senator, and representative to state and local positions, the political endorsement of Huston Cobb Jr. was very desirable.

Not only was Huston Cobb Jr. sought after by political candidates, but he was also asked and agreed to serve on prestigious boards of local importance to northwest Alabama. Mr. Cobb served on the Board of Trustees at the University of North Alabama in Florence. In addition, Huston was on the Board of Equalization for Colbert County for many years. Huston Cobb Jr. preformed his public service duties with utmost distinction.

In the 1980s, Huston realized the importance of recording the history of his Black neighbors and kinfolks who were descendants of local slaves that lived in the Town Creek Triangle and surrounding areas of Colbert County and northwest Alabama. He visited many Black elders in the area and recorded their personal family stories. Through the efforts of Huston Cobb Jr., a treasure trove of historically significant information that would have been lost forever was saved.

Huston was influenced to record historical information of the Black community by Alexander "Alex" Haley who wrote the 1976 book *Roots: The Saga of an American Family*; Haley also wrote the 1993 novel *Queen: The Story of an American Family*. Huston and William L. McDonald, a noted local historian, had toured with Mr. Haley when he came to northwest Alabama to investigate the history of his slave ancestors who inspired the two television miniseries.

There are not enough words to describe all the successful accomplishments of Huston Cobb Jr. He has made significant social, historical, and political contributions for both Black and White families of northwest Alabama. But to me, it was an extreme honor and privilege to coauthor *Black Folktales of the Muscle Shoals* with Mr. Huston Cobb Jr.

Rickey Butch Walker